Tom Bowling is a Londoner born ... g family in the Neckinger, a part of Berm... named after the Devil's Neckinger or ... by pirates executed there. He is the author of a late eighteenth-century seafaring novel, *The Antigallican*.

NEW YORK

New Jersey

Hudson River

MANHATTAN

East River

Long Island Sound

LONG ISLAND

Newark Bay

STATEN ISLAND

The Narrows

Jamaica Bay

N
NW · NE
W · E
SW · SE
S

THE MOUTH of the HUDSON RIVER c.1700

A BRIEF HISTORY OF

PIRATES AND BUCCANEERS

TOM BOWLING

ROBINSON   RUNNING PRESS
PHILADELPHIA · LONDON

Constable & Robinson Ltd
3 The Lanchesters
162 Fulham Palace Road
London W6 9ER
www.constablerobinson.com

First published in the UK in 2008 by Pocket Essentials
P.O. Box 394, Harpenden, Herts, AL5 1XJ

This revised and updated edition published by Robinson,
an imprint of Constable & Robinson, 2010

A copy of the British Library Cataloguing in Publication
Data is available from the British Library

UK ISBN 978-1-84901-279-9

1 3 5 7 9 10 8 6 4 2

First published in the United States in 2010
by Running Press Book Publishers

9 8 7 6 5 4 3 2 1

Digit on the right indicates the number of this printing

US Library of Congress Control Number: 2009935106

US ISBN 978-0-7624-3852-5

Running Press Book Publishers
2300 Chestnut Street
Philadelphia, PA 19103–4371

Visit us on the web!

www.runningpress.com

Typeset by TW Typesetting, Plymouth, Devon
Printed and bound in the EU

CONTENTS

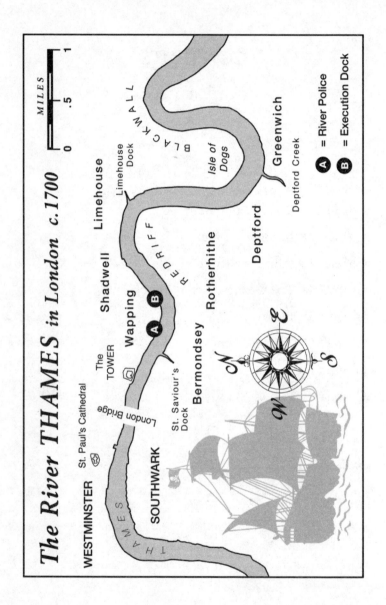

The River THAMES in London c.1700

WESTMINSTER   St. Paul's Cathedral

London Bridge

St. Saviour's Dock

The TOWER   Wapping   Shadwell   Limehouse

REDRIFF

Limehouse Dock

SOUTHWARK

THAMES

Bermondsey   Rotherhithe

Isle of Dogs

BLACKWALL

Deptford

Greenwich

Deptford Creek

A = River Police
B = Execution Dock

MILES
0   .5   1

I

WHAT IS A PIRATE?

A pirate is a sea-robber, an exploiter of weakness. If a pirate has the power he will take what's yours. It's simple. Historically, we see pirate captains as a form of gang leader, pirates as their gang members. But this implies piracy is more than a simple moral failing. Gangs are a social phenomenon. The pirate could be an unfortunate sailor captured and left no choice but to join the 'gang'. He could be a soldier continuing his trade outside the law. He could even be a politician, pursuing a colonial 'policy' by extra-judiciary means. All of these are in the pages which follow.

The high water mark of piracy, the period of the classic buccaneer (never privateer or corsair, as we shall see) with a ring in his ear, tricorn hat, fuses in his hair, cutlass, pistols and buried treasure, the period of the iconic pirate who conformed to all the prejudices we have gained from reading books and watching films, was undoubtedly the seventeenth and early eighteenth centuries.

The place was the Spanish Main, by which I mean the Spanish American empire which stretched from Venezuela around the Caribbean to Florida. In the seventeenth and eighteenth centuries, Florida was a Spanish possession. The Spanish Main included some Caribbean islands. The classic Spanish Main pirate could be black or white, French, Spanish, American, Dutch or English. There are plenty of examples of each. Nor were his activities constrained by national boundaries, except in the case of a privateer, a sort of official, state-sanctioned sea-robber whose exact circumstances we will discuss later.

Just as interesting as the spread of race and nationality, the pirates' 'class' (perhaps too modern a term for this period; 'social background' might be a better description) could not be predicted. There were 'well to do' pirates and, famously, a few women pirates. 'He' could be male or female. He could be black or white. He could come from any one of a dozen seafaring countries. He could terrorize the seas for years or appear, grab a fortune and disappear again. This classic pirate, the one alluded to in the cinema performances of Johnny Depp and Errol Flynn, has gone forever. We have our own pirates now.

Though piracy is thought of as a characteristic of the Caribbean, it took place (and may today take place) around the world in the South China Sea, South America, the Indian Ocean, the Eastern American seaboard, the shores around Britain, even on the Thames and the Hudson rivers. There are plenty of reminders of piracy in London and New York.

I was brought up in a family full of sailors in London. We lived by the side of what had been the river Neckinger in Bermondsey. Notwithstanding the fact that Execution Dock in Wapping lies opposite on the north side of the Thames, the Neckinger is reputed (not least by the Mayor of London's website) to have been named after the Devil's Neckinger, or necktie, by which is meant the hangman's noose. Pirates are said to have been hanged at the Neckinger river mouth. Hence the name, it is implied: a nice story, unless yours were the neck to be stretched.

Certainly it is recorded that convicted pirates' bodies were displayed in chains at Blackwall, Cuckold's Point and Redriff (i.e. Rotherhithe), which are all within a mile of the mouth of the Neckinger. But I've never seen a document which condemns a pirate to be hanged at or by the Neckinger. Though I'd have loved to have seen a pirate gallows there as a boy, though I'm certain there were Thames pirates until just outside living memory, I think the Devil's Neckinger story is showman's puff, a repeated and convenient invention, not history. It also runs contrary to all we know about place names – the names of rivers change immensely slowly and rivers in England usually have their Roman or Ancient British names. How come the Neckinger gained its name during the age of pirates? I don't think it did.

Long before the time of my own childhood the Neckinger river had been entirely culverted and ran under our feet, save for the last couple of hundred yards of its course, which had been turned into St Saviour's Dock. The Neckinger supplied water to Bermondsey's last remaining tannery, then trickled below the tarmac, before running eventually into the Thames and down to the sea.

My grandfather had sailed up the London river, as sailors call the Thames, at the turn of the twentieth century. My father and his brothers sailed in Royal or Merchant Navies (or both) during the 1940s and 1950s. We were a salt-water family. We lived right next to the Pool of London and I often played on the muddy strand below St Saviour's Dock, which is formed from the mouth of the Neckinger river.

As we played, the steel bellies of dried-out ships towered over us, like beached whales. Thames Division coppers came as close as they dared in their launches and bellowed at us through foghorns, 'Get orf the shore.' We didn't. They couldn't enforce their threats, we knew. They would go aground if they came any closer. We were little boys and knew no boundaries and no danger. So, at the mouth of the Neckinger, where pirates were not hanged, we played.

Lacking gallows, nooses, bodies dangling above our heads (oh, how we would have loved them), lacking men with hooked hands and peg legs, lacking bags of bones left in chains, lacking secret maps and treasure chests, lacking any sort of fear or knowledge of piracy, we stumbled about on the grit and mud during the day and learned about pirates later from 'history' and adventure books.

If Thames pirates had existed in the 1950s, we would have known about them, just as plainly as we saw the big beefy London river coppers in their boats. There were no pirates but plenty of coppers. Equally, if there had been common and large-scale piracy in, say, the South China Sea in the 1940s, my father, who had spent that decade sailing around it in a wheezy old tramp steamer, would have known of it and talked about it. But he didn't. He talked about everything else he'd encountered on that trip, one that lasted years and was caused by the ship-owner 'shanghai-ing' his crew which, in the 1940s, meant sending the tramp further and further into the lost reaches of a far-off ocean where they wouldn't have a chance to leave the ship and get home.

In the eighteenth century this might have caused the crew to mutiny, leading to accusations of piracy. Later in the book I've included excerpts from the *Proceedings of the Old Bailey*, which describe exactly this. Being 'shanghaied', as English sailors call it, seems to have been a common reason for men turning pirate. Unlike Teach's, Morgan's, Kidd's or Avery's men, my father and his shipmates belonged to a trade union. His vessel eventually fetched up on the shores of what is now Bangladesh, where the crew struck and were repatriated. But throughout they saw no pirates. The closest any of us, fathers and sons, came to meeting pirates was in our imaginations, a truly distant land.

Today there are pirates in the area between India, Indonesia and Burma. The Chinese government tried a group of them as recently as 2000. According to the *Chinese People's Daily*:

Fourteen Myanmarese[1] pirates were charged with raiding a Taiwanese cargo ship and setting its 21 crew members adrift in the Andaman Sea. The pirates hijacked the Marine Master cargo ship in the small hours of March 17, 1999, which was sailing through the Andaman Sea south of Myanmar, heading from China's eastern port of

Zhangjiagang to Calcutta, India, when the pirates boarded the ship. Armed with guns and knives, the pirates hijacked the ship and seized alkali as well as crew members' valuables with a total value of more than 5.8 million yuan (US$698,000). The crew was forced into a lifeboat, which floated for 10 days before being rescued by fishermen from Thailand. Meanwhile, the pirates disguized the cargo ship and sailed it to the port of Shantou in south China's Guangdong Province, where they sold the cargo of alkali. When the ship arrived at the city of Fangchenggang in Southern Guangxi for repairs on June 8, local police spotted it and arrested the pirates.

The pirate leader was sentenced to death, the others to long terms of imprisonment. The account of the robbery could come straight from the accounts of the Admiralty courts of the eighteenth century. The Andaman Sea is the body of water between Burma and India. Burma by western standards is lawless, and lawlessness, often the result of wars, is one of the necessary conditions for piracy.

It hasn't always been necessary to travel to far off places in search of pirates. Marlowe's comment on the Thames in Conrad's *Heart of Darkness* ('this also, has been one of the dark places of the earth') compared Romans to the Belgians on the Congo, but it might well have applied to Africans enslaved and taken to the New World a hundred years earlier, say to Chesapeake or to New York's Hudson river (the Hudson Valley Institute suggests 15 per cent of farms in that region were worked by African slaves in 1776). Holding a man or woman as a slave and treating them as property was without moral or legal foundation then as now. Lawlessness is a requisite of piracy.

A boy in Brooklyn or Bermondsey might have seen pirates for himself in the eighteenth and nineteenth centuries, when there was undoubtedly organized piracy on the Thames and on the New York Hudson and East rivers. Pirates exploited what was essentially a lawless environment. So the presence of pirates in London and New York led to the formation of the first police forces.

The river piracy losses these police forces were formed to prevent were enormous, running into many hundreds of thousands of pounds sterling. Net public expenditure for Britain in 1798 was £64,000,000, so losses on the Thames of, say, half a million pounds would represent a sum approaching 1 per cent of the national budget. At today's prices 1 per cent of, for example, 2005 UK government expenditure would be of the order of £2,770,000,000 sterling.

Eighteenth-century Thames pirates were organized in gangs known, with economy of vocabulary, as 'River Pirates' and 'Mudlarks'. The nineteenth-century New York rivers had several groups of pirates, the most important being known as the Hole-in-the-Wall gang. This was 20 years before Butch Cassidy and his co-criminals were in a gang of the same name and the two gangs are not related. The London River Police were formed in 1798. These anti-pirate river police were the very first proper, state-run police force in England, predating the formation of the Metropolitan Police by 30 years. The denizens of London were disgusted by the move. The new River Police, with their fast rowboats full of constables armed with muskets and cutlasses, were considered a hugely dangerous and illiberal extension of the state, yet another revolting and interfering idea brought from Europe, where the French Revolution was in full swing.

Soon after the River Police were established, a crowd estimated to be 2,000 strong demonstrated outside their rented offices in Wapping and tried to burn the building down. The Thames River Pirates and Mudlarks were making off with half a million pounds' worth of goods a year, though. They had to be stopped. What a quandary! Sometimes it's possible to get the feeling nothing ever changes in the English psyche.

It's tempting to view pirates as the extreme, radical edge of free market economics. We still talk of free marketeers as having a 'buccaneering'[2] spirit, with no real sense of criticism attached. It may be from this sense that we derive the modern usage of a pirate as someone who breaks market rules (for example, on copyright, at an internet site like http://thepiratebay.org/).

It may also be that our definition of 'pirate' needs re-examining. The behaviour characteristic of pirates can be seen elsewhere in society. Men who prey on others, who live by their own outsider moral code, who move with speed and offer violence are common enough. Pirates fill a power vacuum left by the state. The term might be applied to Dick Turpin and the Gregory Gang in eighteenth-century England (they even tortured their victims, pirate style) or to Jesse James and the James gang in nineteenth-century USA. For that matter, it might be applied to any of the other groups of men who made the West wild in the years immediately after the American Civil War. The sheer distances and scarcity of population in America before mass immigration in the late nineteenth century meant that large areas of the country had no real government.

A pirate needs lawlessness, weapons, victims, the ability to move quickly. A pirate needs a viable 'outsider' society. A pirate needs cash or valuables to prey upon. Does a pirate need a boat? Probably. But having a boat doesn't make a pirate. Raphael Semmes is sometimes referred to as 'the Confederate pirate' when he was nothing of the sort. He was the captain of a Confederate commerce raider during the American civil war and a former officer of the US Navy. He was a rebel and took his ship, the *Alabama*, on a world tour of destruction of Union shipping; he sunk or captured over 60 Union ships – but he was neither a pirate nor a corsair. That's a different matter.

If the James gang and their like were the land-based pirates of the developing west of the United States, they had plenty of counterparts in the east. The rivers around Jersey, New York, Staten Island and Long Island abounded with pirates in the early part of the nineteenth century. The New York River Police were formed to counter them in 1858. It was none too soon.

Before New York gangsters had cars, they had boats. In the early nineteenth century, river pirates from New York City travelled in rowboats and attacked not only ships at anchor but country houses and country people on Long Island, the rural Jersey shore and in the Hudson Valley. Such were the depredations farmers suffered from Manhattan gangsters marauding the waterways that, on the Jersey shore at least, they had been reduced to meeting anyone landing from a boat with gunfire. These water-borne New York gangsters, like those in London, fulfil any conceivable definition of 'pirates' – they travelled by water, they were armed and they committed crimes of either theft or violence or both.

Like death and taxes, pirates have always been with us. Mediterranean pirates, either Corsican or Barbary, Balearic or Cretan, had existed back into the depths of history. Julius Caesar himself was held prisoner by Cilician (southern Turkish) pirates in 75 BC. According to Plutarch:

> ... when the pirates demanded a ransom of 20 talents, Caesar burst out laughing. They did not know, he said, who it was that they had captured, and he volunteered to pay 50. Then, when he had sent his followers to the various cities in order to raise the money and was left with one friend and two servants among these Cilicians, about the most bloodthirsty people in the world, he treated them so highhandedly that, whenever he wanted to sleep, he would send to them and tell them to stop talking.
>
> For 38 days, with the greatest unconcern, he joined in all their games and exercises, just as if he was their leader instead of their prisoner. He also wrote poems and speeches which he read aloud to them, and if they failed to admire his work, he would call them to their faces illiterate savages, and would often laughingly threaten to have them all hanged. They were much taken with this and attributed his freedom of speech to a kind of simplicity in his character or boyish playfulness.

However, the ransom arrived from Miletus and, as soon as he had paid it and been set free, he immediately manned some ships and set sail from the harbour of Miletus against the pirates. He found them still there, lying at anchor off the island, and he captured nearly all of them. He took their property as spoils of war and put the men themselves into the prison at Pergamon. He then went in person to Junius, governor of Asia, thinking it proper that he, as praetor in charge of the province, should see to the punishment of the prisoners. Junius, however, cast longing eyes at the money, which came to a considerable sum, and kept saying that he needed time to look into the case. Caesar paid no further attention to him. He went to Pergamon, took the pirates out of prison and crucified the lot of them, just as he had often told them he would do when he was on the island and they imagined that he was joking.

Pirates, as we shall see, did not always have things their own way. Perhaps the Cilician pirates (we don't have their names) would have been best served by moving on and counting their money elsewhere. Caesar was clearly interested in maritime matters – he notes elsewhere that the Veniti (the inhabitants of Vannes in modern Brittany) used chain for their anchors. It must have been an expensive system to manufacture by the standards and with the technology of the period but would resist either pirates or Romans stealing the ships.

Though there was piracy in the early twentieth century, and there is undoubtedly piracy now, the 1940s, 1950s and 1960s seem to have been peculiarly clear of it. Why? The clues might be in maritime power, fast outboard engines and the development of the United Nations. After the Second World War the victorious allies had a surfeit of naval power. They were capable, at least at sea, of enforcing international law. This law doesn't only govern states and their dealings with each other but also authorizes states' forces to protect their citizens no matter where they are in the world. After the Second World War western states felt they had both power and the right to use it, at least within a legal framework.

This is a question of self-belief. In the 1940s the forum for regulation of international behaviour was being established – the UN. Briefly both the will and the method of enforcing the forum's will were reaching a high-water mark. The UN had been conceived as a kind of parliament of nations, the Nuremberg trials suggested a world community which sets a legal limit to tyranny, or at least implies the possibility of retribution against tyrants. The world became briefly more hopeful and lawful, as has happened in the recent past with the trials of Slobodan Milosevic and Charles Taylor in The Hague. They were both pirate leaders of demoralized, immoral and chaotic states leading forces which raped, robbed and murdered with, they thought, impunity.

I'm sure it's clear by now that I believe piracy is associated with state lawlessness and poverty. If the state does not or cannot care for its citizens it has no moral right to rule. In these circumstances a moral vacuum develops which is filled by desperate, dangerous or simply greedy men. If the men had jobs and a proper legal structure to live by, they would be too busy to be pirates. Daniel Defoe (or was it he?[3]) in *Captain Johnson's General History of the Pyrates* has a view on the matter:

I cannot but take Notice in this Place, that during this long Peace, I have not so much as heard of a *Dutch* Pyrate: It is not that I take them to be honester than their Neighbours; but when we account for it, it will, perhaps, be a Reproach to our selves for our want of Industry: The Reason I take to be, that after a War, when the *Dutch* Ships are laid up, they have a Fishery, where their Seamen find immediate Business, and as comfortable Bread as they had before. Had ours the same Recourse in their Necessities, I'm certain we should find the same Effect from it; for a Fishery is a Trade that cannot be overstock'd; the Sea is wide enough for us all, we need not quarrel for Elbow-room: Its Stores are infinite, and will ever reward the Labourer. Besides, our own Coast, for the most Part, supply the *Dutch*, who employ several hundred Sail constantly in the Trade, and so sell to us our own Fish. I call it our own, for the Sovereignty of the *British Seas, are to this Day acknowledged us by the Dutch*, and all the neighbouring Nations; wherefore, if there was a publick Spirit among us, it would be well worth our while to establish a National Fishery, which would be the best Means in the World to prevent Pyracy, employ a Number of the Poor, and ease the Nation of a great Burthen, by lowering the Price of Provision in general, as well as of several other Commodities.

I need not bring any Proofs of what I advance, viz. that there are Multitudes of Seamen at this Day unemploy'd;

it is but too evident by their straggling, and begging all over the Kingdom. Nor is it so much their Inclination to Idleness, as their own hard Fate, in being cast off after their Work is done, to starve or steal. I have not known a Man of War commission'd for several Years past, but three times her Compliment of Men have offer'd themselves in 24 Hours; the Merchants take their Advantage of this, lessen their Wages, and those few who are in Business are poorly paid, and but poorly fed; such Usage breeds Discontents amongst them, and makes them eager for any Change. I shall not repeat what I have said in the History concerning the Privateers of the West-Indies, where I have taken Notice they live upon Spoil; and as Custom is a second Nature, it is no Wonder that, when an honest Livlyhood is not easily had, they run into one so like their own; so that it may be said, that Privateers in Time of War are a Nursery for Pyrates against a Peace.

Now we have accounted for their Rise and Beginning, it will be natural to enquire why they are not taken and destroy'd, before they come to any Head, seeing that they are seldom less than twelve Men of War stationed in our American Plantations, even in Time of Peace; a Force sufficient to contend with a powerful Enemy. This Enquiry, perhaps, will not turn much to the Honour of those concern'd in that Service; however, I hope I may be excus'd, if what I bint is with a Design of serving the Publick.

I say, 'tis strange that a few Pyrates should ravage the Seas for Years, without ever being light upon, by any of our Ships of War; when in the mean Time, they (the Pyrates) shall take Fleets of Ships; it looks as if one was much more diligent in their Affairs, than the other. Roberts and his Crew, alone, took 400 Sail, before he was destroy'd.

Piracy needs both the moral vacuum and the poverty in order to exist. It is no coincidence that the worst areas for piracy today include the Horn of Africa, where there has been a seemingly endless war since the 1970s; the seas around Colombia and Venezuela, where a drugs war rages; and, of course, South East Asia, where the defeat of the United States in the Vietnam War led to just such a power vacuum (superpower vacuum in this case) and where many territories are still in rebellion against their central government. This is the case of the Aceh insurgency. When the 2005 tsunami struck, Indonesian soldiers were wary about going into Aceh. As well they might be, since Jakarta's writ does not run there. For Indonesian armed forces, Sumatra, Java and Aceh are bandit country. People there are poor and a man might be a peasant one day, a fisherman the next and a pirate on the third. He has to eat.

Sumatran and Javan sea piracy, let loose in the 1970s as the US reeled back from the disaster of Vietnam War, is now allied to all sorts of anti-state, anti-Western groupings. Of course, however poorly states are run they are usually preferable to the kind of *ad hoc* semi-judicial arrangements outlaw societies impose on their members and their victims. You wouldn't look to pirates for justice.

The 'legal' arrangements from the pirates' point of view are quite simple: at a certain point in time and geography, you have money or goods and the pirate does not. He has weapons, you do not. He has a group of loyal companions who will help enforce his will, you do not. This is happening in Iraq, in Afghanistan, in Indonesia and the Horn of Africa, in Nigeria, in the Palestinian territories . . . There are as many brigands and pirates in the world now as there ever were. As Brecht put it, in his play *The Resistible Rise of Arturo Ui*, 'the bitch that bore him is in heat again.'

Of course, I do not imply that, because I haven't heard of it, there was no piracy in the middle of the twentieth century. I'm sure there was. I expect rather that it was at a level which didn't allow it to reach the consciousness of those of us in England or, for that matter, in New England. We were safe. The huge navies deployed by both the British and Americans in the middle of the twentieth century no doubt helped secure us. British pragmatism, buying off those who could be bought off, fighting those who couldn't, would have finished the job in the 1940s just as it did in the 1840s. Were there pirates off Aden in the 1940s? There are none of whom I can find any record. Why were there none? I think the chances of encountering an American or British warship ready to shoot was too high for piratically inclined young men to take the risk.

And there's the question of speed and power, because all the circumstances need to be right for a pirate to exist. He needs it to be worth his while – in other words there must be vessels or waterside communities grossly richer than himself to prey upon, he needs the power to enforce his will (i.e. cheap weapons) and he needs to feel he can get away. The pirate, whether he is a twentieth-century African or an eighteenth-century Englishman, needs a fast ship. There are of course other complementary conditions to piracy – the existence of an outlaw culture, the lack of proper lawful behaviour by states, perhaps a lack of opportunity or education within the state; but the main conditions are simple and direct – the pirate must have ready victims, he must stand to gain money, he must have cheap power and a fast vessel. He must find weaknesses to exploit, which means he must have access to information. The traditional Spanish Main pirate knew where the weak points were. He knew which routes ships would be forced to ply (because of trade winds and the limited ability of square-rigged ships to go to windward) and he knew which towns were weakly defended. Speed, power and ruthlessness applied to weak defences produce results and, as we shall see, some pirates and privateers of the past fetched spectacular results.

In the 1940s and 1950s the outboard-motor-driven fast RIB or planing speedboat was yet to become universal. Russian and Chinese guns stayed, by and large, in Russia and China where they were controlled by state military rather than insurgents-cum-robbers. Whatever pirates exis-ted in that period would have found themselves outgunned by navies and most likely outrun by merchantmen. They could not apply enough power and, because merchant ships and even sometimes what yachts there were, moved faster than fishing boats of the period, they were not presented with opportunities.

When Port Said Johnny approached merchant ships in the 1940s he had a sail up and nothing more dangerous than souvenir merchandise or fresh fruit under the covers of his little boat. Nowadays his cousins in the Red Sea might carry Kalashnikovs and be propelled by twin 110 horse-power Hondas.

The sailing website Noonsite (http://www.noonsite.com/General/Piracy) gives the following tips for recognizing contemporary pirates:

Boat Size: Most pirates, whether in the north-western Indian Ocean, off Somalia, or in the region around the Straits of Malacca, are using relatively small boats, essentially the same size as used by the local fishermen. So if a couple of fishing skiffs try to approach you, watch out. And be especially careful if they're moving at a good clip. That's because ordinary fishermen are loath to open up their engines, since fuel is money.

Crew Size: Most fishing boats have at most three crewmen. If there are more than that in a boat, or nearby in several boats, it's likely that someone's up to no good.

Fishing Gear: If you don't spot nets or other equipment associated with fishing, the boat may be looking for bigger game.

Birds: Fishing boats usually are accompanied by little clouds of sea birds; no birds, no fish, and that means pirates.

Fishing Grounds: Even in the relatively undeveloped regions where piracy flourishes, local governments usually maintain websites identifying fisheries, particularly those in their exclusive economic zones. If you spot fishing boats far from any of these, caution would be advised

Weapons: Even if there are only two or three guys in a boat, if they're waving weapons around, it's probably a good idea to avoid them.

It's good advice.

Modern yachts, just like modern container ships, seem grossly rich to the world's poor, of course, and the yachts have the advantage of being usually unarmed and travelling relatively slowly – typically under six knots. They must look like a slow-moving self-service conveyor belt to a poor African. To a man in a fast boat with a Kalashnikov they represent an opportunity. This is no doubt how US and British merchant vessels appeared to pirates at the end of the eighteenth and beginning of the nineteenth centuries; slow moving, poorly armed and richly laden opportunities. But is that all? There may have been an element of cultural combat even then. There certainly had been between the Protestant British and Catholic Spanish in the sixteenth and seventeenth centuries.

One way of characterizing privateering would be as a proxy war. The British, French and Spanish had fought proxy wars against sixteenth- and seventeenth-century pirates in the Caribbean and the Americas, the US fought with African and Arab pirates. The US struggled with piracy from her beginning as a nation. In the 1780s American ships were preyed upon by Barbary (i.e., Moroccan, Tunisian or Algerian) pirates. The US government paid over $60,000 cash and made a treaty with the Moroccans but not the other Barbary states. So Arab corsairs continued their raiding. In 1786 Thomas Jefferson questioned Rahman Adja, the ambassador to Britain from Tripoli, about why his state was so aggressive towards the US, which had done nothing by way of provocation. Adja answered, according to Jefferson, that:

... it was founded on the Laws of their Prophet, that it was written in their Koran, that all nations who should not have acknowledged their authority were sinners, that it was their right and duty to make war upon them wherever they could be found, and to make slaves of all they could take as Prisoners, and that every Musselman who should be slain in Battle was sure to go to Paradise.

This is ominously familiar stuff to readers in the early twenty-first century. As a result of this impossible situation money was voted and the United States Navy was born in March 1794. Six frigates were built, including the USS *United States*, the USS *Constitution* and the USS *Constellation*. The last is still afloat and regularly sailing today. The purpose of these vessels was to defend US merchant interests and trade wherever US vessels ventured. Though the British and Americans were in competition, sporadically at war with each other and at loggerheads over the slave trade, they both tried to suppress piracy throughout the nineteenth century. Of course, the warships were a forceful back-up to diplomacy. 'Speak softly but carry a big stick,' wrote a later US president, Theodore Roosevelt.

The US needed a big stick because it fought a series of formal wars with the Barbary States over what were essentially state-sponsored pirate attacks on its shipping, following failed attempts by Jefferson and others at diplomacy. Other states with interests in the Mediterranean and along the North African coast paid a tribute to the Barbary states as late as the 1830s. By the end of the nineteenth century the British and Americans had to a great extent prevailed. The French and Spanish occupied much of North Africa as colonies. The British controlled the straits of Gibraltar. The slave trade was ended after a bloody war (and various forms of internal piracy) in the USA.

By the beginning of the twentieth century piracy was well suppressed. Now the wheel has turned full circle again. There certainly are contemporary pirates behaving more or less in the classical pirate way. They exist in significant numbers in the Horn of Africa and the seas around Indonesia, particularly the Malaysian Malacca Coast and among the islands between Langkawi and Phuket, Thailand. They exist in Venezuela, Colombia and Brazil. Men in fast boats with cheap machine guns from Russia or China raid ships in these areas weekly. The Red Sea has become a dangerous place if not a virtual no-go area for yachts. Japanese cargo ships report frequent attacks in the seas about Indonesia. Pirates are about.

If my knowledge of polar bear hunts, of being torpedoed by Germans or accidentally run down by Liberty ships came from first-hand eye-witnesses, my idea of a pirate came from books in Spa Road Public Library. What most of us know about pirates, thankfully, is a culturally rendered experience. It's second hand. To me, and probably to you, a pirate meant Blackbeard Teach, or Morgan, Calico Jack or one of those fellows from R.L. Stevenson, stumbling about with a patch over his eye and a black spot in his hand.

These are iconic pirates, the pictures we all hold in our

heads. They are what Disney means by pirates in their theme ride, what is meant by pirate in the Johnny Depp films. We will start with these iconic pirates. To discover them we need to know how they came by their role.

2

BECOMING A PIRATE

In his introduction to Athanase Postel's autobiographical *Memoires d'un Corsaire et Aventurier* (Éditions la Découvrance) Michel Lefevre lists various types of corsair activity:[4] *petit corse* which is coastal and might be undertaken in small ships, harassing another nation's trade vessels and profiting, of course, from its actions (Channel Islanders were famous for making the *petit corse*, a sort of seasonal respite from the long haul to the fishing grounds of the Terre Neuve); *grand corse* which implies travelling long distances in bigger ships (Postel himself went on privateer raids on the British fishing fleets of Iceland and Nova Scotia during his career); and *corse d'etat*, state corsairs, which are no more and no less than privateers in the general sense we know of them – ships armed, fitted out and crewed at the expense of individuals or groups of individuals to do the state's work of war. The great difference between a privateer and a ship of a state's navy is, of course, that the privateer wouldn't usually expect to be so precisely placed in the military chain of command as, say, a Royal Navy frigate. There would be no point in asking a privateer to patrol and blockade Brest for years on end as the British Royal Navy under Lord Howe did during the Revolutionary and Napoleonic Wars. The privateer can only exist from the profits raised by his raiding and there are unlikely to be profits to be made from containing the French Revolutionary navy in Brest. Real money would flow instead from raiding their great trading ships. So privateers or corsairs follow the money.

Lefevre distinguishes usefully between corsairs and 'archipirates'. The latter is a term he uses for the classic 'Spanish Main' type pirates. Unlike corsairs, classic pirates wouldn't give a damn for any state permission to carry on their business – in fact one of their characteristics is that they establish parallel societies. They have rules entirely of their own devising.

As an example of these rules, here is the pirate code attributed to Bartholomew Roberts in 1720:

I. Every man has a vote in affairs of moment; has equal title to the fresh provisions, or strong liquors, at any time seized, and may use them at pleasure, unless a scarcity (not an uncommon thing among them) makes it necessary, for the good of all, to vote a retrenchment.

II. Every man to be called fairly in turn, by list, on board of prizes because (over and above their proper share) they were on these occasions allowed a shift of clothes: but if they defrauded the company to the value of a dollar in plate, jewels, or money, marooning was their punishment. If the robbery was only betwixt one another, they contented themselves with slitting the ears and nose of him that was guilty, and set him on shore, not in an uninhabited place, but somewhere, where he was sure to encounter hardships.

III. No person to game at cards or dice for money.

IV. The lights and candles to be put out at eight o'clock at night: if any of the crew, after that hour still remained inclined for drinking, they were to do it on the open deck.

V. To keep their piece, pistols, and cutlass clean and fit for service.

VI. No boy or woman to be allowed amongst them. If any man were to be found seducing any of the latter sex, and carried her to sea, disguised, he was to suffer death; [so that when any fell into their hands, as it chanced in the Onslow, they put a sentinel immediately over her to prevent ill consequences from so dangerous an instrument of division and quarrel; but then here lies the roguery; they contend who shall be sentinel, which happens generally to one of the greatest bullies, who, to secure the lady's virtue, will let none lie with her but himself.]

VII. To desert the ship or their quarters in battle, was punished with death or marooning.

VIII. No striking one another on board, but every man's quarrels to be ended on shore, at sword and pistol. [The quarter-master of the ship, when the parties will not come to any reconciliation, accompanies them on shore with what assistance he thinks proper, and turns the disputant back to back, at so many paces distance; at the word of command, they turn and fire immediately (or else the piece is knocked out of their hands). If both miss, they come to their cutlasses, and then he is declared the victor who draws the first blood.]

IX. No man to talk of breaking up their way of living, till each had shared one thousand pounds. If in order to this, any man should lose a limb, or become a cripple in their service, he was to have eight hundred dollars, out of the public stock, and for lesser hurts, proportionately.

X. The captain and quartermaster to receive two shares of a prize: the master, boatswain, and gunner, one share and a half, and other officers one and quarter.

XI. The musicians to have rest on the Sabbath Day, but the other six days and nights, none without special favour.

A corsair or privateer, on the other hand, will have a state sanction or other signed and sealed official permit in some form usually described as 'letters of mark' allowing him to raid other shipping. Corsairs did not consider themselves pirates. They stayed inside rules of war, such as existed in their period, and expected to be treated as prisoners of war if captured in their turn. The best a pirate could hope for was the noose.

Athanase Postel went from being a military cadet in Boulogne under the revolutionary government of 1794 to crew member of a corsair raiding British fishing fleets and coastal trade, more or less as a standard step in his career as a military sailor. No such route was available in England and not many French 12-year-olds would want to follow it, but some did, driven by a taste for adventure. Louis Garneray (*Mes Voyages, Aventures et Combats*, Editions

La Decouvrance) was the son of a Parisian portrait painter. The family's only connection to the sea was a cousin who was a cadet and, after a conversation with this cousin, Louis travelled from Paris to Dunkirk in search of adventure. He found a post on a sailing ship and ended up striding the decks of a frigate in the Indian Ocean beside Robert Surcouf, the most famous corsair of the revolutionary war period.

Surcouf is a romantic figure, a man who ran the British ragged in the Indian Ocean and made himself immensely rich into the bargain. 'La Grande Corse' with Surcouf in the Indian Ocean fully satisfied the young Garneray's need for adventure. However romantic a figure he cut, Surcouf had his dark side too. Before the revolution he had been a slaver, transporting unfortunate Africans to a life of misery in America and the Caribbean. Surcouf enriched himself from slavery and enriched his home port, St Malo, from his later adventures as a corsair in the Indian Ocean. (However, he retired to Redon. Perhaps the adulation in the northern port disturbed him. Redon, although it is a salt port, is 40 kilometres inland.)

State sponsorship is what distanced the likes of Surcouf from archipirates. It's what made the life of a corsair possible for rather proper young revolutionary *mousses* (French boy sailors) like Garneray and Postel. What seems to make a man an archipirate in Lefevre's sense is that the state describes him as such. Stede Bonnet (executed in 1718) inherited land in Barbados and lived as a landowner before serving in the island's militia and turning pirate. Perhaps he'd gone mad; people certainly thought so at his trial. In

1709, Bonnet had married Mary Allamby and joined the militia as a major.

In the summer of 1717, perhaps driven by a nagging wife (Mary is accused of being this in some sources), perhaps by a taste for adventure and comradeship the militia offered, Bonnet bought a sailing vessel, named it *Revenge*, and travelled along the American coast wrecking, setting afire and looting vessels which fell into his path. He had become a pirate. According to Defoe/Johnson:

The Major was no Sailor as was said before, and therefore had been obliged to yield to many Things that were imposed on him, during their Undertaking, for want of a competent Knowledge in maritime Affairs; at length happening to fall in Company with another Pyrate, one Edward Teach, (who for his remarkable black ugly Beard, was more commonly called Black-beard). This Fellow was a good Sailor, but a most cruel hardened Villain, bold and daring to the last Degree, and would not stick at the perpetrating of the most abominable Wicked-ness imaginable; for which he was made Chief of that execrable Gang, that it might be said that his Post was not unduly filled, Black-beard being truly the Superior in Roguery, of all the Company, as has been already related.

To him Bonnet's Crew joined in Consortship, and Bonnet himself was laid aside, notwithstanding the Sloop was his own; he went aboard Black-beard's Ship, not concerning himself with any of their Affairs, where he continued till she was lost in Topsail Inlet, and one Richards was appointed Captain in his Room. The Major now saw his Folly, but could not help himself, which made him Melancholy; he reflected upon his past Course of Life, and was confounded with Shame, when he thought upon what he had done: His Behaviour was taken Notice of by the other Pyrates, who liked him never the better for it; and he often declared to some of them, that he would gladly leave off that Way of Living, being fully tired of it; but he should be ashamed to see the Face of any English Man again; therefore if he could get to Spain or Portugal, where he might be undiscovered, he would spend the Remainder of his Days in either of those Countries, otherwise he must continue with them as long as he lived.

When Black-beard lost his Ship at Topsail Inlet, and surrendered to the King's Proclamation, Bonnet reassumed the Command of his own Sloop, Revenge, goes directly away to Bath-Town in North-Carolina, surrenders likewise to the King's Pardon, and receives a Certificate. The War was now broke out between the Tripple Allies and Spain; so Major Bonnet gets a Clearence for his Sloop at North-Carolina, to go to the Island of St. Thomas, with a Design (at least it was pretended so) to get the Emperor's Commission, to go a Privateering upon the Spaniards. When Bonnet came back to Topsail Inlet, he found that Teach and his Gang were gone, and that they had taken all the Money, small Arms and Effects of Value out of the great Ship, and set ashore on a small sandy Island above a League from the Main, seventeen Men, no doubt with a Design they should perish, there being no Inhabitant, or Provisions to subsist withal, nor any Boat or Materials to build or make any kind of Launch or Vessel, to escape from that desolate Place: They remained there two Nights and one Day, without Subsistance, or the least Prospect of any, expecting nothing else but a lingering Death; when to their inexpressable Comfort, they saw Redemption at Hand; for Major Bonnet happening to get Intelligence of their being there, by two of the Pyrates who had escaped Teach's Cruelty, and had got to a poor little Village at the upper End of the Harbour, sent his Boat to make Discovery of the Truth of the Matter, which the poor Wretches seeing, made a signal to them, and they were all brought on Board Bonnet's Sloop.

Major Bonnet told all his Company, that he would take a Commission to go against the Spaniards, and to that End, was going to St. Thomas's therefore if they would go with him, they should be welcome; whereupon they all consented, but as the Sloop was preparing to sail, a BomBoat, that brought Apples and Sider to sell to the Sloop's Men, informed them, that Captain Teach lay at Ocricock Inlet, with only 18 or 20 Hands. Bonnet, who bore him a mortal Hatred for some Insults offered him, went immediately in pursuit of Black-beard, but it happened too late, for he missed of him there, and after four Days Cruize, hearing no farther News of him, they steered their Course towards Virginia.

In the Month of July, these Adventurers came off the Capes, and meeting with a Pink[5] with a Stock of Provisions on Board, which they happened to be in Want of, they took out of her ten or twelve Barrels of Pork, and about 400 Weight of Bread; but because they would not have this set down to the Account of Pyracy, they gave them eight or ten Casks of Rice, and an old Cable, in lieu thereof.

Two Days afterwards they chased a Sloop of sixty Ton, and took her two Leagues off of Cape Henry; they were so happy here as to get a Supply of Liquor to their Victuals, for they brought from her two Hogsheads of Rum, and as many of Molosses, which, it seems, they had need of, tho' they had not ready Money to purchase them: What Security they intended to give, I can't tell, but Bonnet sent eight Men to take Care of the Prize Sloop, who, perhaps, not caring to make Use of those accustom'd Freedoms, took the first Opportunity to go off with her, and Bonnet (who was pleased to have himself called Captain Thomas) saw them no more.

After this, the Major threw off all Restraint, and though he had just before received his Majesty's Mercy, in the Name of Stede Bonnet, he relaps'd in good Earnest into his old Vocation, by the Name of Captain Thomas, and recommenced a down-right Pyrate, by taking and plundering all the Vessels he met with: He took off Cape Henry, two Ships from Virginia, bound to Glascow, out of which they had very little besides an hundred Weight of Tobacco. The next Day they took a small Sloop bound from Virginia to Bermudas, which supply'd them with twenty Barrels of Pork, some Bacon, and they gave her in return, two Barrels of Rice, and a Hogshead of Molossus; out of this Sloop two Men enter'd voluntarily. The next they took was another Virginia Man, bound to Glascow, out of which they had nothing of Value, save only a few Combs, Pins and Needles, and gave her instead thereof, a Barrel of Pork, and two Barrels of Bread.

The depredations of 'Captain Thomas' on American shipping continued until the end of the month:

The last Day of July, our Rovers with the Vessels last taken, left Delaware Bay, and sailed to Cape Fear River, where they staid too long for their Safety, for the Pyrate Sloop which they now new named the Royal James, proved very leaky, so that they were obliged to remain here almost two Months, to refit and repair their Vessel: They took in this River a small Shallop, which they ripped up to mend the Sloop, and retarded the further Prosecution of their Voyage, as before mentioned, till the News came to Carolina, of a Pyrate Sloop's being there to carreen with her Prizes. Upon this Information, the Council of South-Carolina was alarmed, and apprehended they should receive another Visit from them speedily; to prevent which, Colonel William Rhet, of the same Province, waited on the Governor, and generously offered himself to go with two Sloops to attack this Pyrate; which the Governor readily accepted, and accordingly gave the Colonel a Commission and full Power, to fit such Vessels as he thought proper for the Design.

In a few Days two Sloops were equipped and manned: The Henry with 8 Guns and 70 Men, commanded by Captain John Masters, and the Sea Nymph, with 8 Guns and 60 Men, commanded by Captain Fayrer Hall, both under the entire Direction and Command of the aforesaid Colonel Rhet, who, on the 14th of September, went on Board the Henry, and, with the other Sloop, sailed from Charles-Town to Swillivants Island, to put themselves in order for the Cruize. Just then arrived a small Ship from Antigoa, one Cock Master, with an Account, that in Sight of the Bar he was taken and plundered by one Charles Vane, a Pyrate, in a Brigantine of 12 Guns and 90 Men; and who had also taken two other Vessels bound in there, one a small Sloop, Captain Dill Master, from Barbadoes; the other a Brigantine, Captain Thompson Master, from Guiney, with ninety odd Negroes, which they took out of the Vessel, and put on Board another Sloop then under the Command of one Yeats, his Consort, with 25 Men. This prov'd fortunate to the Owners of the Guiney Man, for Yeats having often attempted to quit this Course of Life, took an Opportunity in the Night, to leave Vane and to run into North-Edisto River, to the Southward of Charles-Town, and surrendered to his Majesty's Pardon. The Owners got their Negroes, and Yeats and his Men had Certificates given them from the Government.

Vane cruised some Time off the Bar, in hopes to catch Yeats, and unfortunately for them, took two Ships coming out, bound to London, and while the Prisoners were aboard, some of the Pyrates gave out, that they designed to go into one of the Rivers to the Southward. Colonel Rhet, upon hearing this, sailed over the Bar the 15th of September, with the two Sloops before mentioned; and having the Wind Northerly, went after the Pyrate Vane, and scoured the Rivers and Inlets to the Southward; but not meeting with him, tacked and stood for Cape Fear River, in Prosecution of his first Design. On the 26th following, in the Evening, the Colonel with his small Squadron, entered the River, and saw, over a Point of Land, three Sloops at an Anchor, which were Major Bonnet and his Prizes; but it happened that in going up the River, the Pilot run the Colonel's Sloops aground, and it was dark before they were on Float, which hindered their getting up that Night. The Pyrates soon discovered the Sloops, but not knowing who they were, or upon what Design they came into that River, they manned three Canoes, and sent them down to take them, but they quickly found their Mistake, and returned to the Sloop, with the unwelcome News. Major Bonnet made Preparations that Night for engaging, and took all the Men out of the Prizes. He shewed Captain Manwaring, one of his Prisoners, a Letter, he had just wrote, which he declared he would send to the Governor of Carolina; the Letter was to this Effect, viz. That if the Sloops, which then appeared, were sent out against him, by the said Governor, and he should get clear off, that he would burn and destroy all Ships or Vessels going in or coming out of South-Carolina. The next Morning they got under Sail, and came down the River, designing only a running Fight. Colonel Rhet's Sloops got likewise under Sail, and stood for him, getting upon each Quarter of the Pyrate, with Intent to board him; which he perceiving, edged in towards the Shore, and being warmly engaged, their Sloop ran a-ground: The Carolina Sloops being in the same shoal Water, were in the same Circumstances; the Henry, in which Colonel Rhet was, grounded within Pistol shot of the Pyrate, and on his Bow; the other Sloop grounded right a-head of him, and almost out of Gun-Shot, which made her of little Service to the Colonel, while they lay a-ground.

At this Time the Pyrate had a considerable Advantage; for their Sloop, after she was a-ground, listed from Colonel Rhet's, by which Means they were all covered, and the Colonel's Sloop listing the same Way, his Men were much exposed; notwithstanding which, they kept a brisk Fire the whole Time they lay thus a-ground, which was near five Hours. The Pyrates made a Wiff in their bloody Flag, and beckoned several Times with their Hats in Derision to the Colonel's Men, to come on Board, which they answered with chearful Huzza's, and said, that they would speak with them by and by; which accordingly happened, for the Colonel's Sloop being first afloat, he got into deeper Water, and after mending the Sloop's Rigging, which was much shattered in the Engagement, they stood for the Pyrate, to give the finishing Stroke, and designed to go directly on Board him; which he prevented, by sending a Flag of Truce, and after some Time capitulating, they surrendered themselves Prisoners. The Colonel took Possession of the Sloop, and was extreamly pleased to find that Captain Thomas, who commanded her, was the individual Person of Major Stede Bonnet, who had done them the Honour several Times to visit their own Coast of Carolina.

There were killed in this Action, on Board the Henry, ten Men, and fourteen wounded; on Board the Sea Nymph, two killed and four wounded. The Officers and Sailors in both Sloops behaved themselves with the greatest Bravery; and had not the Sloops so unluckily run aground, they had taken the Pyrate with much less loss of Men; but as he designed to get by them, and so make a running Fight, the Carolina Sloops were obliged to keep near him, to prevent his getting away. Of the Pyrates there were seven killed and five wounded, two of which died soon after of their Wounds. Colonel Rhet weigh'd the 30th of September, from Cape Fear River, and arrived at Charles-Town the 3rd of October, to the great Joy of the whole Province of Carolina.

Bonnet and his Crew, two Days after, were put ashore, and there not being a publick Prison, the Pyrates were kept at the Watch-House, under a Guard of Militia; but Major Bonnet was committed into the Custody of the Marshal, at his House; and in a few Days after, David Hariot the Master, and Ignatius Pell the Boatswain, who were designed for Evidences against the other Pyrates, were removed from the rest of the Crew, to the said Marshal's House, and every Night two Centinals set about the said House; but whether thro' any Corruption, or want of Care in guarding the Prisoners, I can't say; but on the 24th of October, the Major and Hariot made their Escape, the Boat-swain refusing to go along with them. This made a great Noise in the Province, and People were open in their Resentments, often reflecting on the Governor, and others in the Magistracy, as tho' they had been brib'd, for conniving at their Escape. These Invectives arose from their Fears, that Bonnet would be capable of raising another Company, and prosecute his Revenge against this Country, for what he had lately, tho' justly, suffered: But they were in a short Time made easy in those Respects; for as soon as the Governor had the Account of Bonnet's Escape, he immediately issued out a Proclamation, and promised a Reward of 700 Pounds to any that would take him, and sent several Boats with armed Men, both to the Northward and Southward, in pursuit of him.

Bonnet stood to the Northward, in a small Vessel, but wanting Necessaries, and the Weather being bad, he was forced back, and so return'd with his Canoe, to Swillivants Island, near Charles-Town, to fetch Supplies; but there being some Information sent to the Governor, he sent for Colonel Rhet, and desired him to go in pursuit of Bonnet; and accordingly gave him a Commission for that Purpose: Wherefore the Colonel, with proper Craft, and some Men, went away that Night for Swillivant's Island, and, after a very diligent Seach, discovered Bonnet and Hariot together; the Colonel's Men fired upon them, and killed Hariot upon the Spot, and wounded one Negro and an Indian. Bonnet submitted, and surrender'd himself; and the next Morning, being November the 6th, was brought by Colonel Rhet to Charles-Town, and, by the Governor's Warrant, was committed into safe Custody, in order for his being brought to his Tryal.

So ended the pirate's career. The devious and incompetent Bonnet was considered completely mad by many of his contemporaries, but he was a pirate and died as such, with a certain amount of notoriety. Perhaps the real source of his notoriety (and prominence in Defoe's book) is his relationship with Edward Teach, or Blackbeard, famous for his bloodthirstiness and for terrifying his victims with his multiple weapons and burning fuses in his hair. Some of his contemporaries thought he was the devil incarnate. It seems we can't get enough of Blackbeard, surely the greatest archipirate. We will meet him again.

What made a man a pirate was first and foremost society's view of him. The possessor of *lettres marques*, striding the quarterdeck of a warship fitted out by speculative businessmen (the equivalent of fishing boat *armateurs* or shipowners) at the behest of the state, was most certainly not a pirate, as we have seen, though it might be noted that the revolutionary and terrorist government in Paris in the 1790s, while quick to cut off the heads of those who opposed it, was squeamish and slow about awarding Surcouf *lettres marques*. They thought they shouldn't associate their revolution with corsairs. Everyone has his own standards. Soon practicalities overcame the revolutionary government when ships' captains began quitting their posts. There was a mutiny in Quimper. Eventually, by the end of the Terror, the revolutionary government of France was only too pleased to appoint Surcouf, or Charleston corsairs or whoever else was skilled in the seas and willing to take their cause.

They had meanwhile executed or alienated able ships' captains and experimented with merchant seamen as captains of warships. JeanBon St André, the government's special representative to the marine service (i.e. Navy Minister) was a former priest and merchant seaman and clearly had a higher opinion of the abilities of merchant seamen than some of the military captains. At least he'd given up the church, otherwise he might have put priests at the helm. None of it worked, and when Surcouf presented himself as a raider on British shipping there must have been a sigh of relief among French naval chiefs.

What made a man a Stede Bonnet, a Blackbeard or a Captain Kidd was circumstance and his own character. What made an ordinary seaman a pirate (in the sense of being a crew member on a pirate ship) was often simple circumstance too. Often the only way of resisting a cruel, criminal or insane captain was to take over the ship, considered in the eighteenth and nineteenth centuries as a form of mutiny. Modern sailors would get on the satphone or VHF radio and complain to the owner. Sailors of an earlier period had either to bear the unfairness, danger and cruelty or, if it became intolerable, to take the ultimate risk of wresting control from the god-like figure on the quarterdeck – the captain. In his turn the captain's easiest defence to charges of cruelty, criminality or insanity would, of course, be to counter-accuse his crew of becoming pirates. The certainty of just such an accusation might well tip the balance . . . the crew might as well *behave* as pirates if they were to *hang* as pirates. In fact, a crew containing a mad, avaricious or power-hungry dominant personality could easily be tipped into mutinying against even a good captain. Perhaps it was lack of fresh food, or poor conditions, or homesickness. Perhaps it was the drink, or lack of it, but what is certain is that some members of crews would sometimes rebel, 'turn pirate' following some strong-minded individual, and this would leave non-piratically inclined fellows in a difficult situation to either turn pirate with the others or die.

Even a man who would prefer to keep his own counsel might be later accused of being part of a conspiracy in piracy. There are many examples of crews getting into this sort of fix, but perhaps a sanguine examination of the problem is contained in the report of the trial in 1737 of Richard Coyle, domiciled, appropriately enough, in St Olave's parish, which is to say that, when ashore, he lived by the sides of the river Neckinger in Bermondsey. Coyle took part in a conspiracy to take over his ship, the pink *St John*, off Padras, then in Turkey, now in Peloponnesian Greece. His co-conspirator in mutiny and piracy and co-accused was the American ship's carpenter John

Richardson. According to the *Newgate Calendar*, at least, Richardson had a thoroughgoing career as thief, seducer, conman and ne'er-do-well. Perhaps Richardson was the mad, avaricious or power-hungry dominant personality every mutiny needs. However, he was the carpenter, whereas Coyle was the first officer, and the trial of Coyle is what gives us a great insight into the events on the pink *St John*.

Coyle was tried twice at the Old Bailey for murder and piracy (pirates were held at the Marshalsea prison in Southwark and the trials were held by the Admiralty wherever it was convenient; for example, the Admiralty Session following the trial of Coyle at the Bailey was held in the Doctor's Commons,[6] an ecclesiastical court dedicated to civil law which was between St Paul's Cathedral and the Thames). Incompetence and drunkenness are of course key characteristics of pirates, and Coyle and his companions had those qualifications in spades. If Coyle and his crew hadn't been so incompetent the men of the *St John* would undoubtedly have become fully blown pirates. It is interesting to see the counter-accusations the crewmen laid against each other. You wouldn't expect any love lost between mutineers and murderers and there was none.

From *Proceedings of the Old Bailey*:

> Counsel. My Lords, and you Gentlemen of the Jury; the Prisoner at the Bar stands indicted on two Indictments; the First is, for the Murder of his Captain; the other is for Piracy. We shall proceed on the Murder first, and not

meddle with the Piracy, 'till you have the Evidence on that Head, laid before you. The Case will come out thus, – This Ship, the St. John Pink, belonged to Yarmouth, and one Benjamin Hartley was Master. In January 1733, this Ship went from Yarmouth to Leghorn, loaden with Herrings; when she arrived at Leghorn; she was employed to trade from Port to Port in the Mediterranean. On the 25th of August 1735 the Master of this Ship, departed from Padras in Turkey, loaden with Corn, and bound for Leghorn. The Ships Company was the Prisoner Coyle, Larson, a Dutchman, Richardson the Carpenter, and Davison the Cook; four Mariners besides the Master. There was also three Apprentices to the Master, then on Board, Philip Wallis, William Durrant, and William Metcalf. The Day after the Ship sailed from Padras, about two in the Morning, the Apprentices Wallis and Durrant, were asleep, or laid down in a Place call'd the Cable-Teer, a Place, I presume, where the Cables are deposited; they hearing a Shriek, and a great Noise went up on Deck, and there they saw the Master, in the Fore-shrouds of the Ship, endeavouring to avoid the Danger that threaten'd him, and begging his Life. I would aggravate a Case of this Nature, but will leave the Captain's Expressions to come before you from the Witnesses. They had at this Time a Blunderbuss among them, and they endeavoured to shoot him with it, but (I think) it missed firing. After this, the Prisoner at the Bar, as we apprehend, took hold of the Captain to throw him over-board into the Sea, but he holding by the Lanniards (a Part of the Ship which will be explained to you) the Prisoner took up a Hen-coop Trough, and struck him with it, in order to beat him off, into the Sea, but his

Blows had not the wish'd for Effect. The Captain held fast, and did not fall into the Sea, so another of the Confederates, which we have not yet got, the Carpenter Richardson, he struck him on the Head with an Axe, and his Blows were so effectual, that the Captain fell off, into the Sea and was drowned. The Fact is attended with such aggravated Circumstances of Cruelty, that I must leave the rest, to come from the Witnesses themselves. After they had committed this Murder, they ran away with the Ship, but as this more properly belongs to the Piracy, for which the Prisoner is likewise indicted, I shall only mention the Manner in which they were taken.

The Prisoner at the Bar, after the Captain was murdered, took upon him the Command of the Ship, and wanting fresh Provision, about fifteen Days afterwards they came to Foviniano, an Island belonging to the Crown of Spain, and here, tho' they wanted Provision, yet, being sensible of their Guilt, they were afraid to go on Shore, but sent Messages ashore to and fro in the Night, and one Night while the rest were asleep, the Apprentices, who were not so materially concerned, took an Opportunity of getting ashore, and gave Information to the Magistrates, of the Fact which had been committed: The Crew remaining on board, finding the Boys were gone on Shore, thought it best for them to run away, so they all quitted the Ship, and shifted from Place to Place, till at last the Prisoner was taken at Tunis, and was brought hither.

Philip Wallis was call'd and sworn.

Wallis. On Monday in the Forenoon ('twas the 26th of August to the best of my Knowledge, 1735) The

Morning of that Day we came out of the Harbour, and that Night between one and two, they began to murder the Captain; I heard nothing of it till the Captain came up upon Deck, and then I saw the Dutchman Larson, jump down and hand up two Blunderbusses, one of them he gave to the Prisoner, and he (the Prisoner) went towards the Captain, who was then upon the Fore-Shrouds, crying out, dear Mr. Coyle, what are you against me?

Counsel. And what did the Prisoner say?

Wallis. He said, yes, he was, and told the Captain it was a Thing consulted among all the Ship's Company, and that over-board he must go, and over-board he should go. After this, the Captain called out to Richardson the Carpenter, – my dear Carpenter, are you against me too? No Sir, says he, I am not, and immediately he and the Dutchman followed the Captain up the Shrouds into the Fore-top; the Captain ran up the Shrouds into the Fore-top, and the Dutchman and the Carpenter followed him.

Counsel. Had they any Weapons in their Hands?

Wallis. The Carpenter had a Broad Axe, and the Dutchman had a Blunderbuss. The Captain cry'd out to them, For Christ's Sake, – for God Almighty's Sake spare my Life! I will hurt none of you, if you'll spare my Life! The Dutchman asked him, whether he would forgive him? and the Capt. said, yes, if you'll spare my Life, and he put out his Hand to shake Hands with him, but Richardson, who followed the Dutchman, said, G – d d – n you, if you offer to shake Hands with him, I'll chop your Hands off.

Counsel. Where was the Prisoner at this Time?

Wallis. He was below with a Blunderbuss, and said nothing at all just then: But Richardson told the Dutchman, if he offer'd to shake Hands with the Captain, he would clive [cleave] him down the Head. Then the Captain begg'd again, that they would remember his Wife and Family, and the Prisoner call'd out and said, G – d d – n you why don't you fetch him down? Why do you stand talking to him? As we have begun, we must go through with it. Then the Captain got from them to the Fore-mast, and Coyle and the other two got hold of him and flung him over the Gang-way, but he catch'd hold of the Lanniards of the Main Shrouds, and cry'd out to us, Boys, Boys, can't you do something for me! We said we could not; one of my Fellow-Servants got hold of me and said, Let us save the Captain's Life; but they said they would knock us down if we offer'd to stir. Then the Carpenter got hold of an Axe, and knock'd his Brains out. The Prisoner took up the Chicken Trough to strike him with, but I cannot say I saw him strike; tho' he was close by when Richardson knock'd the Captain into the Sea with his broad Axe.

Counsel. When they had kill'd the Captain, what follow'd?

Wallis. After that they went down into the Captain's Cabbin, and broke open his Scrutore.

Counsel. Who did?

Wallis. Richardson broke it open, and what Things they found they put by themselves together: There was no

Money on Board: Then they loaded all the Arms in the Ship.

Counsel. What did they do that for?

Wallis. Coyle and the Dutchman would have them down to load them, because, they said, they could not tell who they had to trust to.

Counsel. After the Death of the Captain, where did you sail to?

Wallis. The first Land we made, afterwards, was the Island of Malta; but before they went to Land, they made Articles, and Richard Coyle the Prisoner was made Captain; Richardson went for Mate, and Larson the Dutchman for Boatswain. Then they came to us, and wanted us to sign the Articles, but we were not willing; so, upon our refusing, they would not go to Land, but Coyle cry'd out, if they won't, – then bear away Boys, we'll remember them another Time; we'll give them nothing but Bread and Water, and serve them worse than the Captain was serv'd. This he said to me and my Fellow-Servants.

Another witness, Metcalf, takes up the story.

Metcalf. The Carpenter told us, if we would not sign it, he would send us the same Way with the Captain. No, says the Prisoner, we'll keep the Ship out at Sea, as long as there's a bit of Beef, or a Drop of Water on Board, and we'll starve them; then we sign'd the Paper, and as soon as we had done it, the Prisoner and the Carpenter laugh'd, and said, now we are sure of you. Then we were coming down the Streights, and after we came between the Island of Mauritimo and Cape Bonne, we stood away to the North ward, and bore away for the Island of Foviniano. They talked of going to Trepany, but Coyle said, 'twas better to go to Foviniano, because there they were not so strict in their Quarantine. When we came to Foviniano, we let out two Anchors, and the Governor in the Morning sent a Man on Board. The Prisoner dress'd himself in the Captain's Cloaths, and he pass'd for Captain, and we went on shore to sell some Corn, and purchase fresh Provisions; but they would take no Corn, and we had no Money, so they could get nothing but Water there. We were kept on Board all the Time, that the Prisoner was on shore; when he return'd to the Ship, he took the Captain's Watch and his silver Spoons, to see if the Governor would take them for Provision, and this Time Davison and Richardson and I, went with the Prisoner on shore, and we took some Casks with us and return'd with Water.

Counsel. And what happen'd next?

Metcalf. In the Night, when they were asleep, I went down and called my Fellow-Servants, and the Greek, and we got into the Yaul, and then we row'd to shore. The Soldiers upon shore, charged us to keep off; but we begg'd for God's sake we might come on shore, and we told them our Captain was Murder'd: Upon this, they suffer'd us to land, and put us all into a Cave for that Night. When the Governor examin'd us, we desir'd 4 Hands to go on Board the Ship, lest they should cut the Cable, or sink the Ship; but after he had examin'd us, he went to his own House, and set 20 or 30 Soldiers over us in the Cave, and they told us they could see the People in the Ship, hauling the Boat a long side of her. We begg'd them to fire a Musket upon them, but they said, they could not Fire without Orders from the Governor; but when they got into the Boat, they Fired 20 or 30 Muskets upon them, but they got away; I saw them go off in the Boat, and never saw any of them since, 'till I saw the Prisoner here.

Coyle's story is rather different.

I have no one to appear for me, nor any Friend, therefore I hope you will hear me patiently. We sail'd from Leghorn, March 23d. When we arriv'd at Messina, we took in Goods and went to a Bay near Syracusa: After that, when we came to Sail, the Captain had some Words with Larson, the Boatswain, about making fast the stopper of the Anchor; the Boatswain got hold of the Captain, and I turn'd my self about, and took him (the Boatswain) by the Collar, and said, Caleb, What are you about to do Mischief? Wallis, one of the Boys said, D – n him, heave him overboard; but I released the Captain out of the Boatswain's Hands, and he went upon the Quarter-Deck. I said to Caleb, go after the Captain, and fall upon your Knees and beg his Pardon: Accordingly he did so, and the Captain forgave him: So we proceeded on our Voyage from thence to the Morea, and we landed some Passengers at Salonica; we were loaded with Tobacco, and were to go from thence to Ancona. I was offer'd a Ship, but the Captain perswaded me to stay with him; no better Agreement could be between two

People, than between him and me; nor did I ever Eat or Drink worse than he himself. When we had made this Voyage, the Captain designed to come Home to Falmouth for Pilchards, upon which 2 Greeks we had a Board desired to be Discharged, he paid them their Wages, and ask'd me if I wanted Money; I told him, it would be more agreeable to me, on account of my Wife and Family, to take my Money at Leghorn. So the Captain paid the Greeks off and Discharged them, and this Richardson, Larson, and the Spaniard came on board in their stead. We then sail'd for Padras, with Money on Board, which the Captain had receiv'd for Freight, and Money receiv'd at Leghorn. We took in a Cargo at Leghorn, and in the Time of loading there, this was express'd by these three young Gentlemen; there was a fine Sloop come from Venice of 160 Tons, which the Carpenter and these Witnesses, and the Spaniard, and the Greek had agreed to cut away in the Night; I heard a great deal of their Villany; – but the Sloop sailing, they were disappointed in their Design. Then, we being loaded sail'd about 8 o' Clock in the Morning, the 11th of August. They took all my Papers, and suffer'd me to save nothing, but what I brought upon my Back out of the Ship. In the Night I went to watch from 8 to 12; they came to call me, so I went upon the Deck, and there I found the Carpenter, the Boatswain, and the Spaniard, I can't say where the Boys were, I believe they might be in the Steerage, but the Carpenter says to me, Coyle, – if you don't take this broad Axe in your Hand and stand at the Cabbin Door, and if the Captain offers to come up, if you don't knock him on the Head I will cut you in Pieces. I said, pray don't do so; if you make a Word on't says he, I'll throw you over-board: So I thought best to take the Axe into my Hand, but when they were gone I threw it down again, and knew nothing of it 'till the Captain came running up upon Deck, and they follow'd him. I ran round and got upon the Quarter-Deck, then I saw the Captain on the Fore-top, and the Carpenter and the Boatswain on the Fore-yard. The Carpenter was an ill Man, I did not like him, – he had not been aboard a Month, – therefore I had no Commerce with him. But I seeing the Captain on the Fore-top, I jumped into the Steerage, and took up a Blunderbuss; but I never loaded it, and I believe there had not been a Pistol nor a Blunderbuss loaded for some Time, for we had not a Pound of Powder on Board. I went for the Blunderbuss to shoot the Carpenter, and being very much surpriz'd, I snapp'd it, (but did not know whether 'twas loaded or not,) with a Design to shoot the Carpenter on the Starboard Side of the QuarterDeck. Metcalf and Durrant brought the Captain round, and I thought they were going to heave him over board. They know I have declared these Things before, and that makes them such strong Evidences against me now. I came round with my Blunderbuss, to strike in among them, I don't know I struck, but it was taken out of my Hands and thrown over board. The Carpenter took the Captain, he struggled, but there was never a Blow struck, nor a Drop of Blood spilt. The Carpenter made a Reach at me with his Axe, and said G – d D – n you, you shall go first, which made me withdraw on the Quarter Deck; then he fetch'd the Captain a Blow, but it did not stun him, so he call'd out to me, Coyle, Coyle, for God's sake help me; Lord have Mercy on you, says I, the Men are all against you, and so they hove him over board. Then Wallis went down into the Cabbin, and brought up 2 Case Bottles, a Bottle of Brandy, and a Bottle of Rack, and they propos'd to make Punch Royal, that is, with Wine in it. Next Morning I said to Wallis what a Piece of Work is this! D – n him, says he, 'twere no Matter if one half of the People at Yarmouth was serv'd in the same Manner. Before the Consul of Tunis, he acknowledged himself guilty, and accused every one of them but me.

Q. When the Captain was kill'd, who navigated the Ship?

Coyle. I did, under the Command of the Carpenter.

Q. Pray why did you leave the Ship?

Coyle. After they went from Foviniano, they differ'd in their Opinions, and were afraid of one another, so the Boys took the Boat unknown to the other Men and went away; when the Boatswain found the Boys and the Boat was gone, he call'd the Carpenter, who lay in the Captain's Cabbin, and told him the Yaul was gone: I was pleased with it, thinking they would now go away and leave me on Board; so the Carpenter turn'd out, and call'd the Spaniard Davison, and they consulted together, and haul'd up the Long Boat, and put Masts and Sails into her, and took what Things of mine were on Board, and then the Carpenter came to me with two or three Cutlasses, and haul'd me on Deck, and said G – d D – n you, get into the Boat; I heard what they were about, and was in Hopes they would have left me in the Ship, so I said, for God's sake don't kill me, and while I was dressing, one of them gave me two or three Blows with the flat side of his Cutlass, and told me, if I would not go he would cut me in Pieces; then he ordered me into the Boat, and put me to an Oar, and one of them steer'd; we row'd a Mile, and got to Windward of the Island, then they ask'd me, what Place they might go too where there was no English Consul; I told them they must go to Tunis or Tripoly: They said they would not go either to Tunis or Tripoly; so after some few Days, we proceeded to a Place just off Tunis, and there we stopp'd to shelter our selves, for the Wind blew hard, and we were loaded: Then we proceeded to Byzarta, and landed 15 Leagues to the Westward of Tunis, and the Carpenter before we put in made me swear, that I would be one of his Company, and said I should not stir from him; he said he would run his Knife thro' me if I spoke any Thing of this Affair. When he came ashore, he was dress'd in the Captain's Cloaths, and appear'd very grand. He told the People he was born in New-York, and pass'd an Examination before the Governor, but what he said there I don't know; but a Paper was brought us, and we all sign'd it. After a while we had all Orders to come to Tunis, so we came to Tunis, and there I was confin'd with the Carpenter, who was Captain for two Days; at last I discover'd the Thing, and the Carpenter made his Escape, but was retaken; the Boatswain turned Turk, and the other turn'd Jew; I was kept in Prison there three Months.

So ended Coyle and Richardson's inept attempt at piracy. The *Proceedings of the Old Bailey* notes laconically, 'The Jury withdrew, and in a short Time returned, and found the Prisoners guilty. Death.'

There is more to this story though. The *Newgate Calendar* reports John Richardson's career prior to joining the *St John*. He is an interesting character:

John Richardson was an American, having been born in the city of New York, where he went to school till he was fourteen years old: he was then put under the care of his brother, who was a cooper; but, not liking that business, he sailed on board a merchant ship, commanded by his namesake, Captain Richardson. After one voyage, he served five years to a carpenter; but having made an illicit connexion with his master's daughter, who became pregnant, he quitted his service, and entered on board a ship bound to Jamaica; on his arrival there he was impressed, put on board a man of war, and brought to England. The ship's crew being paid at Chatham, he came to London, took lodgings in Horsleydown, and spent all his money. [Horsleydown is also in Bermondsey. It's the area where horses and cattle were grazed and is also the site of the extinct Southwark fair. Now the name of a street, Horsleydown more or less corresponds with the area around what is now the southern side of Tower Bridge – in other words less than a quarter of a mile from the Neckinger. When on dry land these men didn't wander far from the sea.] On this he entered as boatswain on board a vessel bound to the Baltic; but, being weary of his situation, he soon quitted that station, having first concerted and executed the following scheme of fraud. Knowing that there was a merchant in the country with whom the captain had dealings, he went to a tavern, and wrote a letter, as from the captain, desiring that the merchant would send him a hundred and six dollars. This letter he carried himself, and received the money from the merchant, who said he had more at the captain's service if it was wanted. Being possessed of this sum, he, the next day, embarked on board a Dutch vessel bound to Amsterdam; and soon after his arrival connected himself with a woman whose husband had sailed as mate of a Dutch East India ship. With this woman he cohabited about eight months, when she told him that it would be necessary for him to decamp, as she daily expected her husband to return from his voyage.

Richardson agreed to depart, but first determined to rob her; and, having persuaded her to go to the play, he took her to a tavern afterwards, where he plied her with liquor till she was perfectly intoxicated. This being done, he attended her home, and, having got her to bed and found her fast asleep, he took the keys out of her pocket, and, unlocking the warehouse, stole India goods to the amount of two hundred pounds, which he conveyed to a lodging he had taken to receive them. He then replaced the keys; but, finding some that were smaller, he with those opened her drawers, and took out sixty pounds. Some years afterwards he saw this woman at Amsterdam, but she made no complaint of the robbery; by which it may reasonably be supposed that she was afraid her husband might suspect her former illicit connexion.

Having put his stolen goods on board one of the Rotterdam boats, he departed for that place, where he found the captain of a vessel bound to New England, with whom he sailed at the expiration of four days. On their arrival at Boston, Richardson went to settle about fifty miles up the country, in expectation that the property he possessed might procure him a wife of some fortune. Having taken his lodgings at a farmer's, he deposited his goods in a kind of warehouse. It being now near the Christmas holy-days, many of the country people solicited that he would keep the festival with them. These offers were so numerous, that he scarce knew how to determine; but at length accepted the invitation of a Mr Brown, to which he was influenced by his having three daughters, and four maid-servants, all of them very agreeable young women. Richardson made presents of India handkerchiefs to all the girls, and so far ingratiated himself into their favour that in a short time all of them were pregnant. But before this circumstance was discovered there happened to be a wedding, to which the daughter of a justice of the peace was invited as a bridesmaid, and Richardson as a bridesman. Our adventurer, soon becoming intimate with the young lady, persuaded her to go and see his lodgings and warehouse, and offered to make her a present of any piece of goods which she might deem worth her acceptance. At length she fixed on a piece of chintz, and carried it home with her. Two days afterwards Richardson wrote to her; and, her answer being such as flattered his wishes, he likewise wrote to her father, requesting permission to pay his addresses to the daughter. The old gentleman readily admitted his visits, and, at the end of three months, gave his consent that the young people should be united in wedlock.

As there were no licenses for marriage in that country, it was the uniform custom to publish the bans three successive Sundays in the church. On the first day no objection was made; but on the second Sunday all the girls from the house where he had spent his Christmas made their appearance to forbid the bans, each of them declaring that she was with child by the intended husband. Hereupon Richardson slipped out of the church, leaving the people astonished at the singularity of the circumstance; but he had reason to suppose that it would not be long before he should hear from the father of the young lady, whom he had already seduced.

Accordingly, in a few days he received a letter from the old gentleman, begging that he would decline his visits, as his conduct furnished a subject of conversation for the whole country; and with his request Richardson very cheerfully complied; but in about four months he was sent for, when the justice offered him 300L. currency, to take his daughter as a wife. He seemed to hesitate at first; but at length consenting, the young lady and he went to a village at the distance of forty miles, where the bans were regularly published, and the marriage took place, before the other parties were apprised of it. However, in a little time after the wedding, he was arrested by the friends of the girls whom he had debauched, in order to compel him to give security for the maintenance of the future children; on which his father-in-law engaged that he should not abscond, and paid him his wife's fortune. Having thus possessed himself of the money, and being sick of his new connexion, he told his wife and her relations that, not being fond of a country life, he would go to New York and build him a ship, and would return at the expiration of three months. The family, having no suspicion of his intentions, took leave of him with every mark of affection; but he never went near them any more.

Having previously sent his effects to Boston, he went to that place, where he soon spent his money amongst the worst kind of company, and, no person being willing to trust him, was reduced to great distress. It now became necessary that he should work for his bread; and, being tolerably well skilled in ship-building, he got employment under a master-builder, who was a Quaker, and who treated him with the greatest indulgence. The Quaker was an elderly man, who had a young wife, with whom Richardson wished to be better acquainted: he therefore one day quitted his work and went home to the house; but he had but just arrived there when he was followed by the old man, who came in search of him, and found him talking to his wife. The Quaker asked him what business he had there, and why he did not keep at his work. Richardson replied that he only came home for an auger: to which the Quaker said, Ah! friend John, I do not much like thee; my wife knows nothing of thy tools, and I fear thou hadst some evil thoughts in thy head.

Hereupon Richardson went back to his work without making any reply, but soon afterwards demanded his wages. The Quaker hesitated to pay him, hinting that he was apprehensive his wife had paid him already; on which Richardson said he would sue him for the debt, and desired him to consider that, if he made such an excuse in open court, he would be disgraced through the country.

On this the Quaker paid his demand, but absolutely forbade him ever to come within his house again; Richardson promising to obey, and intending to have complied with the injunction. About eight days afterwards, the old gentleman, having some business up the country to purchase timber, desired his young wife to accompany him, to prevent any ill consequences that might arise in his absence. To avoid this journey, the lady feigned indisposition, and took to her bed. The husband had not been long gone before Richardson, meeting the maid-servant in the street, asked after the health of her mistress, who, the girl said, wanted to see him; and he promised to wait upon her about nine in the evening. Punctual to his engagement he attended the lady, and renewed his visits to her till the return of her husband was apprehended, when he broke open a chest, stole about seventy pounds, and immediately agreed with Captain Jones for his passage to Philadelphia. When he arrived at the last-mentioned place, he took lodgings at the house of a widow who had two daughters; and, paying his addresses to the mother, he was so successful, that for four months, while he continued there, he acted as if he had been master of the house.

After this intimacy with the mother had continued some time, he became attached to one of the daughters; and on a Sunday, when the rest of the family were absent, found an opportunity of being alone with her; but the mother, returning at this juncture, interrupted their conversation, and expressed her anger in the most violent terms. Nor was this all, for when she was alone with the offender she severely reproached him; but he made his peace by pretending an uncommon attachment to her; yet within a month she found him taking equal freedoms with her second daughter. Upon this the mother became outrageous, and told him that the consequence of his connexion with the other girl was, that she was already pregnant. Richardson now quarrelled in his turn, and told her that if her daughter was breeding she must procure her a husband, for he would have nothing to do with her.

At length, when the old woman's passions were in some degree calmed, he represented to her the impossibility of his marrying both her daughters; but said that, if she could procure a husband for one of them, he would take the other. The old lady soon procured a young man to marry one of her daughters, and then constantly teazed Richardson to wed the other, which he steadily refused to do unless she would advance him a sum of money. She hesitated for some time; but at length said she would give him a hundred pounds, and half her plate; on which he consented, and the marriage was solemnized; but he had no sooner possessed himself of this little fortune than he embarked on board a ship bound for South Carolina.

Within a month after his arrival in this colony he became acquainted with one Captain Roberts, with whom he sailed as mate and carpenter to Jamaica, and during the voyage was treated in the most friendly manner. The business in Jamaica being dispatched, they returned to Carolina.

The owner of the ship living at some distance up the country, and the winter advancing, the captain fixed on Richardson as a proper person to sleep on board and take care of the vessel. This he did for some time, till about a week before Christmas, when he was invited to an entertainment to be given on occasion of the birthday of his owner's only daughter. A moderate share of skill in singing and dancing recommended Richardson to the notice of the company, and in particular to that of the young lady, by which he hoped to profit on a future occasion.

In the following month it happened that a wedding was to be celebrated at the house of a friend of the owner, on which occasion Richardson was sent for; and when he appeared the young lady welcomed him wishing that he would oblige the company with a dance; to which he replied, that he should he happy to oblige the company in general, and her in particular.

Richardson, having been a partner with the young lady during the dancing at the wedding, begged leave to conduct her home; and, when the ceremonies of the wedding were ended, he had the honour to attend her to her abode. When they had got into the midst of a thick wood he pretended to be ill, and said he must get off his horse and sit down on the ground. She likewise dismounted, and they walked together under the shade of a chestnut tree, where they remained till the approach of evening, when he conducted her home, after having received very convincing proofs of her kindness. Going to his ship for that night, he went to her father's house on the following day, and found an opportunity of speaking to her, when he entreated her to admit of his occasional visits; but she said there were so many negro servants about the house that it would be impossible. On this he said he would conduct her to the ship when the family were asleep; and the girl foolishly consenting to this proposal, the intrigue was carried on for a fortnight, when she became so apprehensive of a discovery that she would go no longer. But the lovers being uneasy asunder, they bribed an old female negro, who constantly let Richardson into the young lady's chamber when the rest of the family were retired to rest. At length the mother discovered that her daughter was with child, and charged her to declare who was the father, on which she confessed that it was Richardson. The mother acquainting her husband with the circumstance, the old gentleman sent for Richardson to supper, and, after rallying him on his prowess, told him that he must marry and support his daughter. Richardson said it was out of his power to support her; but the father promising his assistance, the marriage took place.

Soon afterwards the old gentleman gave his son-in-law the ship, and a good cargo, as a marriage portion, and Richardson embarked on a trading voyage to Barbados; but he had not been many days at sea when a violent storm arose, in which he lost his vessel and cargo, and he and his crew were obliged to take to the boat to save their lives.

After driving some days at sea, they were taken up by a vessel which carried them to St. Kitt's, where Richardson soon met with a Captain Jones, who told him that one of his wives had died of a broken heart. This circumstance, added to that of the loss of his ship, drove him distracted; so that he was confined to his chamber for four months. On his recovery he went mate with the captain who had carried him to St. Kitt's; but, quitting this station in about five months, he sailed to Antigua, where a young gentleman, who happened to be in company with Richardson, was so delighted with his skill in dancing a hornpipe, that he invited him to his father's house, where he was entertained for a fortnight with the utmost hospitality. One day, as he was rambling with the young gentleman to take a view of some of the plantations, Richardson stopped on a sudden, and, putting his hand to his pocket, pretended to have lost his purse, containing twenty pistoles. The young gentleman told him there was more money in Antigua. True, said Richardson, but I am a stranger here; I am a Creolian from Nevis. On this the other asked, Do you belong to the Richardsons at Nevis. I know their character well.

Our adventurer, aware that the governor of Nevis was named Richardson, had the confidence to declare that he was his son; on which the other exclaimed, You his son, and want money in Antigua! No, no; only draw a bill upon your father, and I will engage that mine shall help you to the money. The project of raising cash in this manner delighted Richardson; and the young gentleman's father was no sooner acquainted with the pretended circumstance than he expressed a willingness to supply him with a hundred pistoles, on which he drew a bill on his supposed father for the above-mentioned sum, and received the money.

About a week afterwards he wrote a letter to his imputed father, informing him how generously he had been treated by his friends in Antigua, and subscribing himself his 'dutiful son.' This letter he entrusted to the care of a person in whom he could confide, with strict orders not to deliver it; and, when as much time had elapsed as might warrant the expectation of an answer, he employed the mate of a ship to write a letter to the old gentleman, as from his supposed father, thanking him for his civilities to his son. The gentleman was greatly pleased at the receipt of this letter, which he said contained more compliments than his conduct had deserved; and he told Richardson that he might have any farther sum of money that be wanted. On this our adventurer, who was determined to take every advantage of the credulity of his new acquaintance, drew another bill for a hundred pistoles, and soon afterwards decamped.

He now embarked on board a vessel bound for Jamaica, and, on his arrival at Port Royal, purchased a variety of goods of a Jew merchant; which, with other goods that the Jew gave him credit for, he shipped on board a trader to Carthagena, where he disposed of them: but he never went back to discharge his debt to the Jew.

From Carthagena he sailed to Vera Cruz, and thence to England, where he took lodgings with one Thomas Ballard, who kept a public house at Chatham. Now it happened that Ballard had a brother, who, having gone abroad many years before, had never been heard of. Richardson bearing a great resemblance to this brother, the publican conceived a strong idea that he was the same, and asked if his name was not Ballard. At first he answered in the negative; but finding the warm prepossession of the other, and expecting to make some advantage of his credulity, he at length acknowledged that he was his brother. Richardson now lived in a sumptuous manner, and without any expense; and Ballard was never more uneasy than when any one doubted of the reality of the relationship. At length Ballard told Richardson that their two sisters were living at Sittingbourne, and persuaded him to go on a visit to them, to which Richardson readily agreed: the two sisters had no recollection of this man; however, Ballard having persuaded them that he was the real brother who had been so long absent, great rejoicings were made on account of his safe arrival in his native country. After a week of festivity it became necessary for Ballard to return to his business at Chatham: but the sisters, unwilling to part with their newly found brother, persuaded him to remain awhile at Sittingbourne, and told him that their mother, who had been extremely fond of him, had left him twenty pounds, and the mare on which she used to ride; and in a short time he received the legacies.

During his residence with his presumptive sisters he became acquainted with Anne and Sarah Knolding, and, finding that their relations were deceased, and that Anne was left guardian to her sister, he paid his addresses to the former, who was weak enough to trust him with her money, bonds, writings, and the deeds of her estate. Hereupon he immediately went to Chatham, where he mortgaged the estate for three hundred pounds, and thence went to Gravesend, where he shipped himself on board a vessel bound for Venice.

On his arrival at that place he hired a house, and lived unemployed till he had spent the greater part of his money; when he sold off his effects and went to Ancona, where he became acquainted with Captain Benjamin Hartley, who had come thither with a lading of pilchards, and on board whose ship was Richard Coyle, the other offender mentioned in this narrative.

Both Hartley the pilchard carrier and his mate Coyle would soon have reason to regret they had ever met this MacHeath character Richardson. Both paid with their lives. Their contemporary in Early Georgian London John Gay couldn't have written a better criminal character than the ship's carpenter and serial conman, and Coyle's version of events aboard the *St John* doesn't seem so absurd in the light of the rest of Richardson's life story. At the very best, Coyle was under the ship's 'carpenter's' orders. Coyle had conspired with a man we would describe as a form of highly manipulative psychopath[7] without the tools to either recognize Richardson's behaviour nor resist his ensnaring. Even modern prison psychologists cross check with each other after spending a day in the prison company of such characters, such is the power their deviant personalities can wield. One wonders how long it took Richardson to weave his web around the other crew members of the *St John*.

If Coyle's trial sounds like rough justice, compare it to the following, presented by Captain Johnson/Defoe as a pirates' mock trial, reported by an eyewitness. Presumably someone present had been in the Bailey and escaped with his life, able to pass on the basic forms and manners of the great court:

The Court and Criminals being both appointed, as also Council to plead, the Judge got up in a Tree, and had a dirty Tarpaulin hung over his shoulder; this was done by Way of Robe, with a Thrum Cap on his Head, and a large Pair of Spectacles upon his Nose. Thus equipp'd, he settled himself in his Place; and abundance of Officers attending him below, with Crows, Handspikes, etc., instead of Wands, Tipstaves, and such like ... The Criminals were brought out, making a thousand sour Faces; and one who acted as Attorney-General opened the Charge against them; their Speeches were very laconick, and their whole Proceedings concise. We shall give it by Way of Dialogue.

Attor. Gen.: 'An't please your Lordship, and you Gentlemen of the Jury, here is a Fellow before you that is a sad Dog, a sad sad Dog; and I humbly hope your Lordship will order him to be hang'd out of the Way immediately ... He has committed Pyracy upon the High Seas, and we shall prove, an't please your Lordship, that this Fellow, this sad Dog before you, has escaped a thousand Storms, nay, has got safe ashore when the Ship has been cast away, which was a certain Sign he was not born to be drown'd; yet not having the Fear of hanging before his Eyes, he went on robbing and ravishing Man, Woman and Child, plundering Ships Cargoes fore and aft, burning and sinking Ship, Bark and Boat, as if the Devil had been in him. But this is not all, my Lord, he has committed worse Villanies than all these, for we shall prove, that he has been guilty of drinking Small-Beer; and your Lordship knows, there never was a sober Fellow but what was a Rogue. My Lord, I should have spoke much finer than I do now, but that as your Lordship knows our Rum is all out, and how should a Man speak good Law that has not drank a Dram ... However, I hope, your Lordship will order the Fellow to be hang'd.'

Judge: '... Hearkee me, Sirrah ... you lousy, pittiful, illlook'd Dog; what have you to say why you should not be tuck'd up immediately, and set a Sun-drying like a Scarecrow? ... Are you guilty, or not guilty?'

Pris.: 'Not guilty, an't please your Worship.'

Judge: 'Not guilty! say so again, Sirrah, and I'll have you hang'd without any Tryal.'

Pris.: 'An't please your Worship's Honour, my Lord, I am as honest a poor Fellow as ever went between Stem and Stern of a Ship, and can hand, reef, steer, and clap two Ends of a Rope together, as well as e'er a He that ever cross'd salt Water; but I was taken by one George Bradley' (the Name of him that sat as Judge,) 'a notorious Pyrate, a sad Rogue as ever was unhang'd, and he forc'd me, an't please your Honour.'

Judge: 'Answer me, Sirrah . . . How will you be try'd?'

Pris.: 'By G— and my Country.'

Judge: 'The Devil you will . . . Why then, Gentlemen of the Jury, I think we have nothing to do but to proceed to Judgement.'

Attor. Gen.: 'Right, my Lord; for if the Fellow should be suffered to speak, he may clear himself, and that's an Affront to the Court.'

Pris.: 'Pray, my Lord, I hope your Lordship will consider . . .'

Judge: 'Consider! . . . How dare you talk of considering? . . . Sirrah, Sirrah, I never consider'd in all my Life . . . I'll make it Treason to consider.'

Pris.: 'But, I hope, your Lordship will hear some reason.'

Judge: 'D'ye hear how the Scoundrel prates? . . . What have we to do with the Reason? . . . I'd have you to know, Raskal, we don't sit here to hear Reason . . . we go according to Law . . . Is our Dinner ready?'

Attor. Gen.: 'Yes, my Lord.'

Judge: 'Then heark'ee you Raskal at the Bar; hear me, Sirrah, hear me. . . You must suffer, for three reasons; first, because it is not fit I should sit here as Judge, and no Body be hanged . . . Secondly, you must be hanged, because you have a damn'd hanging Look . . . And thirdly, you must be hanged, because I am hungry; for, know, Sirrah, that 'tis a Custom, that whenever the Judge's Dinner is ready before the Tryal is over, the Prisoner is to be hanged of Course . . . There's Law for you, ye Dog . . . So take him away Gaoler.'

Those 'dispensing justice' in the second example are the real thing, pirates, with the tables turned for comic effect. There is apparently humour in every 'trade'.

The men in the first, real trial, Richardson and Coyle and their co-conspirators, are would-be pirates who failed at the first real hurdle. All they had managed to do was to murder a transporter of salt fish, and they barely succeeded in that cruel and pathetic crime. Though they were supposedly qualified as sailors they couldn't reach Lisbon without assistance from fishermen. The problem was that, although Richardson had worked his charm on some members of the fourteen-man crew of the St John, he had failed to mesmerize the entire crew. Without the aid of the captain and part of the small crew, Richardson and Coyle were unable to handle the ship, unable to mount a proper guard over their 'prisoners' and unable to formulate a useful plan. Richardson had over-estimated his abilities. He and Coyle were the *sans-pareil* dunces of the would-be pirate world.

So much for failed pirates and incompetent pirates. We will now look at the activities of some of the more successful pirates.

Were honest men ever accused of piracy? Apparently yes, if the following from the *Newgate Calendar* is to be believed:

Captain James Lowrey (a Scotsman) had just returned from Jamaica, with the charge of a West-Indian trader, when about the middle of the month of June, 1751, a remarkable advertisement appeared in the daily papers, with ten signatures thereto, offering a reward of ten guineas for apprehending James Lowry, late master of the Molly, a merchant-ship, lately arrived from Jamaica, who was charged by ten of his crew, with the cruel murder of Kenith Hossack, foremast-man, in his passage home, on the 24th of December last, by ordering his two wrists to be tied to the main-shrouds, and then whipping him till he expired.

To this captain Lowry replied, by charging his crew with depriving him of his command of the said ship, on the 29th of the said month, and carrying her into Lisbon, where the British consul re-instated him in his command, and he sent the ten subscribing men home prisoners; and that he was ready to surrender when a court should be appointed for his trial, which nothing prevented him from doing immediately, but the thoughts of lying in gaol under the detestable name of an inhuman man.

The crew rejoined in another advertisement, that Lowry did not only murder the said Hossack, as appears by the affidavits of the ten subscribers, and sworn before John Russel, Esq., the British consul, at Lisbon, to be by him transmitted to the lords of the Admiralty, but in the said passage, did use Peter Bright and John Grace so cruelly that they died; and still continuing his barbarity, to every man in the ship, broke the jaw-bone and one of the fingers of William Dwight, and fractured the scull of William Wham.

They admitted that they (the subscribers) had been sent from Lisbon to England, by the said British consul; but this was done in consequence of a pretended charge of piracy sworn against them by Lowry . . .

Proceedings of the Old Bailey takes up the story, related from the witness stand by James Gadderar, the mate:

I was chief mate of the ship called The Molly; the prisoner at the bar was captain; we set sail in the year 1750, Oct. 28, from Jamaica, where the ship was bought, for the port of London; the whole of our crew was fourteen: in the afternoon, a little after four o'clock on the 24th of December. I came upon deck to relieve the watch, and found the deceased Kennith Hossack with one hand tied up to the hallyards, and the other to the main shrouds, upon the quarter-deck. When I came to the deceased, he complained he had been pretty much beat.

Q. Did you see him beat?

Gadderar. Then I had not seen him beat: he begged I would let him loose, for he wanted to ease himself: I told him it was not in my power, but I would go and tell the Captain of it; I went down and told the Captain, and he bid me let him loose; I went and let him down, but he was not able to walk forward: the poor man was very weak, and was seemingly very bad, he could stand, and it was as much as he could do; at last the Captain came on deck again and said, D— —n the rascal, seize him up again, and ordered Hunt, I think it was, to do it; he was immediately tied up again, according to his desire: then the Captain took a small rope of an inch or inch and quarter round, and began to beat him with the bite of it.

Q. What do you mean by the bite of the rope?

Gadderar. That is the double of it, as he held the two ends of it in his hand: I saw him beat the deceased a considerable time till tears stood in my eyes: he would now and then take a turn round the deck, and then beat him again: at last the man hung with his head reclin'd, and his knees to the rising of the quarter deck, as if it was to ease himself: then the captain lifted him up by the arm and beat him again.

Q. How long do you think he beat him?

Gadderar. I believe he might be half an hour beating him and walking backwards and forwards, and beating him again, &c.

Q. Whereabouts did he strike him?

Gadderar. He beat him over the head and temples, I saw him beat him above the shoulders several times, my Lord.

Q. After this beating, how did the body appear?

Gadderar. He hung back his head, the prisoner said, Are you shamming Abraham with me? that he said several times.

Q. What did you understand by that expression?

Gadderar. I understood by it, that he thought the deceased was shamming the thing: it is a cant term, I suppose, often made use of. I went down upon the main deck, and was hawling home the starboard sheet of the main-top-sail, when the captain called to me and said, I believe Kennith is dead: I said, I hope not; when I came, I said, he is dead indeed, Sir.

After this, the crew confined the captain to his quarters and took the ship towards Lisbon. They came into distress and were aided by a Portuguese fishing vessel. Gadderar continues.

Captain Lowrey can talk a little Portuguese, he called the pilot down and talked with him; after that the Portuguese came and told the thing in broken English, that he had sent a letter to the Consul: that very day I had been on board the barge, I was acquainted with the place, and not a man of us had been in Lisbon: we dared nor go ashore, nor we could not go on board another ship without product that is leave to go as I was coming on board again from the barge. There was the man of war's boat coming on board.

So the crew of the Molly were arrested for piracy, released after examination in Lisbon and followed their former captain back to London, where they advertised for his arrest. Lowrey, who had returned by land, gave quite a different account:

Prisoner. This William Waum came to me the day the man died, and made complaint, the deceased had stole a note out of his pocket; immediately James Smout and Hunt came to me, and said the deceased had stole a bottle of rum; I immediately said, where is he? they said down below; I found him extreamly drunk, I assure your Lordship, the people hated him he was so bad a man; he used to steal any thing that was put by. The last evidence told me, he had given him a dram; he was a dreadful rascal for stealing from others; the people exclaimed so much against him, swearing and cursing; I desired he might be made fast, and when sober I would enquire into the merits of the case; he was made fast because he should not get at more liquor; I went down into my cabbin, and about five the mate came and told me he wanted to go and ease himself; said I by all means, but make him fast again; for if he gets below he will get more liquor; about a quarter before 6 I asked the mate how the water was, for we had extream bad water; said I, rend the top-sail, and mend the fore-sail; as soon as I gave orders, I saw the deceased kneeling on his knees, on the quarter deck. I said to the mate, why don't you make that man get up, why do you let him lie in that manner; said he, he is got into his old way of shamming it; I said get up, you sir, (he was an extream odd fellow) when I spoke to him the first time, he got up seeming indifferent, which I concluded was from his being so excessive drunk; I came up in about an hour after, I saw him on his knees again, I called to him, why don't you get up, you sir? he made me no answer; I ran over on the other side, and said, if you don't I will swing you up, he then made me no answer; he would some times work, and some times not:

and the same as to speaking. Said I, I will take the crochet-brace to you; I did, after parling with him for sometime; it was about 2 foot long; he was kneeling, I went over on the other side after he was up, the men were then hawling home the main top-sail sheets, then I called to them to come and take a sick man out of the way of the main top-sail hallyards, they not coming brisk enough, I ran to him, his head was hanging over his shoulder foaming at the mouth.

I called out, Lord, have mercy on me, here is a man dead; Gadderar said, he hoped not, said I, I am afraid he is, lend me a knife to cut him down, they not coming over, I took a pen-knife and cut him loose. There never were such a number of men on board a ship in the universe before. I called Mr. Gadderar to look at him; I put him into a cabbin, and wrapped him up in a sail, he never came to life again; about three days after we had both pumps going and so many sick, I believe they had no sleep for two or three days; I went down to Waum, I found him wrapped up in the gibb, with all his cloths on; he said he had been five months in St. Thomas's hospital of the Rheumatism; I said, put off your wet cloaths, and get into your cabbin, and get something; he fell a crying; the next day the people exclaimed against him, saying, he shammed it; I then made him stand at the pumps as usual, and about four in the afternoon I saw him extreamly drunk: I accused him, and asked him, where he got it; there were not a mate nor a man that I could get to do any thing but myself, the mates were determined to be the ruin of me; Waum told me, at last, if he must tell me, he must, he had it of Mr. Roberts the second mate. I called him, and accused him with selling liquor to the people to make them drunk, when the ship was in that condition. The chief mate's behaviour had obliged me to forbid him my cabbin and mess: I went afterwards on the quarter deck; Roberts beat Waum excessively; I said, when he cryed out, what do you beat the man for? He said for confessing he sold rum to him; said I, don't you see the distresses of the ship? Let the man alone; he said he would beat him, by&& G——d, or d——n his eyes; said I, do you know this is disabling the ship to all intents and purposes; he said he would at all events. I had several people drunk and both pumps going, and expecting the ship to go down every minute. I did knock down my second mate with my sist, that I did, for the good of the ship. I told Roberts I saw he was contriving to ruin the voyage; he said he would not be bothered by me in that manner, he gave me a knock, and I fell, he fell with both his knees on my breast, and got his finger in my mouth; I said let me get up; he said he would beat me; I called out, murder! Gadderar came and lifted him up from me, saying, Mr. Roberts, what do you mean by beating the captain; after that Hunt and the rest came crying and said, Lord, Sir, what shall we do if you are lost? For I was the carpenter, the Doctor, and, I hope, I shall make it appear, if it had not been for me, the ship would have been lost. After they took her into possession, another time the chief mate was going to send me home in a Snow; they wanted to take the ship from me, and go to Carolina, and so to have run her on shore, and never to have been called to an account for it. After they took possession of the ship; I advised them to steer for England, and to do nothing for the badness of the voyage; said I, you'll have the change of the moon. Nothing would serve them, but they would wear ship, and steer to the Western Islands; we had no sail but what was extremely bad; they made waste of the provision; I have gone upon deck and found no man there but him at the helm, and he as drunk as an ape; they contrived to ruin the ship, letting the sails beat to pieces, getting a cag of rum up, and staving the head of it out: they cut the main gears, and let the yards come about their heads; when we got near Lisbon, I ordered them to take care of the anchor and cable; they took care of nothing, but always have kept one man at the helm ten hours, and another six: they swear to defend themselves, least they should be tried for Piracy, as I saw they were intending to run away with the ship; they did every thing that was bad.

The court passed verdict and sentence on him in its usual laconic manner. Guilty, Death. The public response to this Lowry who had killed a crewman and accused the others of piracy was revulsion. The *Newgate Calendar* continues the story:

After conviction, Lowry behaved with great apparent courage and resolution, till a smith came to take measure of him for his chains; when he fainted away, and fell on his bed, and was measured while insensible. On his recovery, he said that it was the disgrace of a public exposure that had affected him, and not the fear of death.

On the 25th of March, at half past nine in the morning, the unfortunate convict was brought out of Newgate, to undergo the sentence of the law; on seeing the cart which was to convey him to the gallows, be became pale but soon recovered a degree of serenity of countenance. He had on a scarlet cloak over a morning gown, and a brown wig, of the colour of his eyebrows. His eyes were very bright and piercing, his features regular and agreeable, and by no means evinced the cruelty of his disposition. He was, in stature, about five feet seven inches, very well proportioned, and about forty years of age. His behaviour was quite composed and undaunted. Before the cart was carried a silver oar of a very antique form.

The dreadful procession had not moved many yards, before the populace began to express their indignation at the culprit. Some sailors cried out, Where is your royal oak's foremast? others vociferated, He is shamming Abraham; and with such tauntings and revilings was he drawn to Execution Dock; near which a number of sailors being collected, they poured execrations on his devoted head.

He was then taken out of the cart, and placed upon a scaffold under the gallows, where he put on a white cap. He prayed very devoutly with the ordinary of Newgate, about a quarter of an hour; then giving the executioner his money and watch, the platform fell. After hanging twenty minutes, the body was cut down, put into a boat, and carried to Blackwall, and there hung in chains, on the bank of the Thames.

3

PIRATE OR PRIVATEER?

In this chapter I want to examine the exploits of some successful pirates of the 'golden age', which, for pirates, is considered to run from the middle of the seventeenth century to the middle of the eighteenth; that is, in terms of British history, from the Civil War to the defeat of the Jacobites at Culloden in 1746 and, in terms of American history, from the arrival of the first Quakers in the Massachusetts colony until just a few years before the War of Independence. 'Success' is of course a relative term. Few pirates failed to end their exploits with their neck in a noose, fewer still were afforded the luxury of legal detention in the Admiralty's own prison, the Marshalsea, the infamy of a death carried out with pomp and a priest at Execution Dock, the notoriety of their body hung in made-to-measure chains at Cuckold's Point on the Thames. Those pirates who took a happy retirement, or moved on to another period in their lives, were remarkable for it. The vast majority were killed by disease, by action, by their fellow pirates or by some lawful force wherever they committed their crimes.

This gloomy prospect, of a life and a career skittling towards a ghastly end, makes you wonder what would cause a man (they were almost all men) to take up service under the black flag of piracy. Of course, it might be that pirates' lives were hardly any more risky than anyone else's. Life in the eighteenth century, in general, was nasty, brutish and short. For the pirate it was nastier, shorter and with a violent end always in view. As soon as a sailor stepped over the imaginary line on deck and became a pirate, he knew his life would be counted away in a few months or a few years at best.

Leaving aside the wretches, usually possessing artisanal skills, who were taken with their ships by pirates and left with no choice – join or die – why would an ordinary, intelligent follower of the sea become a pirate? Sailors were poor until the late twentieth century. Lists of sailors' domestic possessions are rare, but the Naval Miscellany[8] details the belongings of a Royal Navy sailor, James Bearcroft, auctioned on HMS *Gloucester* in 1750 at the end of his life for the benefit of his family. This was a traditional way of raising some cash for the family. The deceased was a gunner, in other words a skilled petty officer of such a rank as might be entitled, for example, to have his wife aboard ship. He was an important man in the life of a Royal Navy ship. The possessions – hats, coats, buckles, rum ration, chest, bolster – and his cash (one shilling and nine pence ha'penny) were valued at just over fourteen pounds in total. Fifty years earlier, when the archipirate Henry Avery captured the Great Mughal's treasure from his ships *Fateh Muhammed* and *Ganj-I-Sawai* in the Indian Ocean, each man's share was £1,000 and some gemstones, the better part of a million sterling in value today.[9] A gunner's share would have been proportionately more, perhaps £3,000 or £4,000 sterling – at today's prices worth over £3,000,000. Honest RN gunner James Bearcroft left at most a couple of thousand pounds, by today's standards; Avery's equivalent gunner, whoever he was, was a lottery winner. Pirate Captain Avery returned to England with his gold but neither it, nor he, lasted long. By 1695, he had disappeared.

But Avery's story must have had a powerful effect on early eighteenth-century sailors. Democracy would have had an effect too. Late seventeenth-century British pirates, like Morgan and his men (see below), were survivors of the English Civil War, the first modern conflict which tried to wrest power from a king. Cromwell and Ireton, leaders of the Parliamentary Army in that conflict, fell out with a large number of their soldiers over the issue of democracy. When the war was won the men doing the fighting wanted their say.

On a pirate ship punishments were almost unknown outside of sanctions approved by the crew as a whole, and the structure of the command of the ship was democratic. Pirates, in general, voted for their commander and might even have voted on what to do next. When Morgan carried out a financially unsuccessful raid on Cuba his pirate force voted, for the most part, to join the French pirate Captain l'Olonnais in search of richer pickings. Pirates generally chose to join a ship and, once joined, they signed up for their laws (articles) and had their 'interest' – the ship and her adventures – right before their eyes. This was an extraordinary degree of self-government by the standards of ordinary men in the late seventeenth- and early eighteenth-century world, where they would ordinarily expect to be indentured servants (that is, someone who had sold his services for a period or 'indenture') or day labourers. Ordinary men and women had no access to a vote and could be imprisoned, executed or transported for the slightest offence.

In the early eighteenth-century American colony there were 50,000 Englishmen and women transported for crimes as small as stealing handkerchiefs or a pewter tankard.[10] Ordinary Englishmen knew what fate awaited them for the smallest crime in the latter half of the seventeenth century: gaol, maiming, transportation or death. Could it be that men who had a taste of action, war and democracy during the English Civil War passed on this taste of freedom to the pirates later in the century?

The imminent prospect of death and the near universal poverty in life were the constant companions of an ordinary sailor in the seventeenth or eighteenth centuries. Immense riches would be available to a successful pirate, whether he was a seaman, mate or captain. Piracy must have made a tempting prospect to many an honest man. However, if a man did turn pirate, he would find himself trapped, like the apocryphal monkey with its hand in the jar. The leisure to enjoy the riches a pirate 'earned', save in brief bacchanalias on, say, Madagascar or the Tortugas or

Port Royal, Jamaica, was rare. Quitting the pirate ship with your fortune was impossible, unless the whole pirate crew was to give up the life. And there was always the chance that your crewmates, another pirate ship or even the Royal Navy would pluck your riches, and perhaps even your life, away.

I imagine a prospective pirate's psychological landscape must have been like that of a man on the edge of an affair with an unstable woman (the gender is immaterial, reverse the sexes if it offends you); what follows next may be exciting but will almost certainly end badly soon. Is the prospect of the pleasure so exciting as to make it worth plumbing the depths of the awful come-uppance? Is it braver to follow your heart and take your chances or is it braver or more timid to remain, as most of us do, right where we are? Perhaps piracy attracted men who would today be inveterate gamblers: always hopeful, always ready to consider a loss a near success, always ready to double not quit. Of course gambling existed in the seventeenth and eighteenth centuries but to take a gamble you need a stake. Sailors of the period were so poor the only stake they could play was their lives. Pirates were men who gambled against fate itself, even though the odds were enormously against them. Before the would-be buccaneer there were the examples of men who were successful enough to make the chance seem worthwhile.

If Avery was the most successful pirate in cash terms, the most successful in absolute terms was undoubtedly Sir Henry (Hari) Morgan, who kept his money, retired as Lieutenant Governor of Jamaica and has a rum named after him. Morgan was even knighted.

The English and the Welsh describe Morgan as a privateer. Hispanics have a different view. There are two riders that must be added to criticism of Morgan. Firstly, raping, robbing, pillaging, torturing and setting a civil population to slavery are at once uncivilized and inexcusable. However, that is exactly how the Spanish behaved in every country they conquered. Morgan merely plumbed the same depths. Secondly, Morgan was a young man during the English Civil War. He went to Jamaica as part of the Commonwealth force under General Venables and Admiral Penn which displaced the Spaniards. Morgan was a soldier while Cromwell was Lord Protector, was preferred under the Restoration regime of Charles II and was knighted and invited to offer military advice by the same king. Their contemporary, the poet John Milton, wrote to Black Tom Fairfax (another English Civil War parliamentary soldier, this time a general, who survived the Restoration), 'For what can war, but endless war, still breed?' If you were a Morgan, 'profit and advancement' would seem to be the answer. The Morgans are comparable to those other New World brown-nosers and sometimes privateers, the Carterets (of Jersey and Carolina). What distinguishes the two families is that the Morgans changed horse midstream – they really were parliamentarians and they really became Restoration soldiers. The Channel Islander Carterets were constant Royalists. Somehow, by a mixture of charm, audacity and fearlessness, the former parliamentary soldier and commission-holder Henry Morgan made himself a rich and marriageable British colonial governor and advisor to the king. Morgan was undoubtedly a man of drive and talent.

Is Morgan a pirate, rather than a privateer? There is something undoubtedly dangerous and psychopathic about him. Morgan doesn't seem troubled by conscience at all in the way an ordinary military sailor might be. His story wasn't written up by Captain Johnson (Defoe), whose *General History of the Robberies and Murders of the Most Notorious Pyrates* (1724) attempted to offer something like a comprehensive survey of piracy. Perhaps Captain Johnson/Defoe thought it impolitic to write about his near contemporary Morgan. Perhaps he simply didn't consider Morgan a pirate. If so, he couldn't have read the story told by Morgan's expedition surgeon Alexandre Exquemelin in the Dutch *Die Americaensche Zee-Rovers* (translated to English in 1684). But why wouldn't a man writing a book on pirates read the bestseller of the previous generation? It seems an unlikely text to miss. Exquemelin's *The American Sea Rovers* was *the* eyewitness account of the period, written by a lucid, intelligent and educated man – it would be like writing about Paris in the 1860s without reading the *Journal des Goncourts* or Berlin in the 1940s without consulting William Shirer's or Christabel Bielenberg's work. And repetition of a good story never inhibited an eighteenth-century writer in any other circumstances. Perhaps the complicated nature of Morgan's dealings with official England explains this shyness, even as late as the reign of George I. Though he escaped punishment and found official favour for his adventures, Morgan was no Raphael Semmes or Robert Surcouf. This is his story.

When General Venables and Admiral Penn drove the Spanish out of Jamaica, Henry Morgan was a junior officer in their expedition. By 1660, Morgan's uncle Edward had become Lieutenant Governor of this new colony of Jamaica. Morgan himself would later become Acting Governor. Henry married his cousin Mary, Edward's daughter. Thus are alliances made.

Morgan went on expeditions to Cuba and to Mexico, where he participated in the sacking of Campeche and took Spanish ships as prizes. By the mid-sixties he was on his way to a fortune. In 1663, Henry Morgan sailed with a small fleet to the Gulf of Mexico. They landed and marched to attack and sack the town of Villahermosa. On returning to Frontera – where their ships had been moored – the expedition found the vessels captured by the Spanish. Morgan took possession of two Spanish ships and some canoes and continued south along the coast of Central America. He attacked and sacked Granada (in modern Nicaragua), then returned to Jamaica a rich man. It is said Morgan tortured the inhabitants of the towns he raided to find the location of their treasure. Since the source of this claim is a member of his expedition, it seems reliable. On his return to Jamaica Morgan organized the island's defences. Perhaps he was afraid some Spanish soldier-cum-admiral would return the compliment. Another man might have settled down at this point. Morgan was rich, he had a wife and had prestige and influence in his small world. Instead, in 1668, he took a small army of pirates, both French and English, to invade a second Spanish possession, Cuba. They attacked Puerto del Principe. Today it's called Camagüey and it is the third largest city in Cuba. Alexandre (sometimes called John) Exquemelin, a French member of Morgan's crew, takes up the story:

Captain Morgan had been but two months in these ports of the south of Cuba, when he had got together a fleet of twelve sail, between ships and great boats, with seven hundred fighting men, part English and part French. They called a council, and some advised to assault the city of Havanna in the night, which they said might easily be done, if they could but take any of the ecclesiastics; yea, that the city might be sacked before the castles could put themselves in a posture of defence. Others pro-pounded, according to their several opinions, other attempts; but the former proposal was rejected, because many of the pirates, who had been prisoners at other times in the said city, affirmed nothing of consequence could be done with less than one thousand five hundred men. Moreover, that with all these people, they ought first go to the island De los Pinos, and land them in small boats about Matamona, fourteen leagues from the said city, whereby to accomplish their designs.

Finally, they saw no possibility of gathering so great a fleet, and hereupon, with what they had, they concluded to attempt some other place. Among the rest, one propounded they should assault the town of El Puerto del Principe. This proposition he persuaded to, by saying he knew that place very well, and that being at a distance from sea, it never was sacked by any pirates, whereby the inhabitants were rich, exercising their trade by ready money, with those of Havanna who kept here an established commerce, chiefly in hides. This proposal was presently admitted by Captain Morgan, and the chief of his companions. Hereupon they ordered every captain to weigh anchor and set sail, steering towards that coast nearest to El Puerto del Principe. Here is a bay named by the Spaniards El Puerto de Santa Maria: being arrived at this bay, a Spaniard, who was prisoner aboard the fleet, swam ashore by night to the town of El Puerto del Principe, giving an account to the inhabitants of the design of the pirates, which he overheard in their discourse, while they thought he did not understand English. The Spaniards upon this advice began to hide their riches, and carry away their movables; the governor immediately raised all the people of the town, freemen and slaves, and with part of them took a post by which of necessity the pirates must pass, and commanded many trees to be cut down and laid cross the ways to hinder their passage, placing several ambuscades strengthened with some pieces of cannon to play upon them on their march. He gathered in all about eight hundred men, of which detaching part into the said ambuscades, with the rest he begirt the town, drawing them up in a spacious field, whence they could see the coming of the pirates at length.

Captain Morgan, with his men, now on the march, found the avenues to the town unpassable; hereupon they took their way through the wood, traversing it with great difficulty, whereby they escaped divers ambuscades; at last they came to the plain, from its figure called by the Spaniards La Savanna, or the Sheet. The governor seeing them come, detached a troop of horse to charge them in the front, thinking to disperse them, and to pursue them with his main body: but this design succeeded not, for the pirates marched in very good order, at the sound of their drums, and with flying colours; coming near the horse they drew into a semicircle, and so advanced towards the Spaniards, who charged them valiantly for a while; but the pirates being very dextrous at their arms, and their governor, with many of their companions, being killed, they retreated towards the wood, to save themselves with more advantage; but before they could reach it, most of them were unfortunately killed by the pirates. Thus they left the victory to these new-come enemies, who had no considerable loss of men in the battle, and but very few wounded. The skirmish lasted four hours: they entered the town not without great resistance of such as were within, who defended themselves as long as possible, and many seeing the enemy in the town, shut themselves up in their own houses, and thence made several shots upon the pirates; who thereupon threatened them, saying, 'If you surrender not voluntarily, you shall soon see the town in a flame, and your wives and children torn to pieces before your faces.' Upon these menaces the Spaniards submitted to the discretion of the pirates, believing they could not continue there long.

As soon as the pirates had possessed themselves of the town, they enclosed all the Spaniards, men, women, children, and slaves, in several churches, and pillaged all the goods they could find; then they searched the country round about, bringing in daily many goods and prisoners, with much provision. With this they fell to making great cheer, after their old custom, without remembering the poor prisoners, whom they let starve in the churches, though they tormented them daily and inhumanly to make them confess where they had hid their goods, money, &c., though little or nothing was left them, not sparing the women and little children, giving them nothing to eat, whereby the greatest part perished.

Pillage and provisions growing scarce, they thought convenient to depart and seek new fortunes in other places; they told the prisoners, 'they should find money to ransom themselves, else they should be all transported to Jamaica; and beside, if they did not pay a second ransom for the town, they would turn every house into ashes.' The Spaniards hereupon nominated among themselves four fellow-prisoners to go and seek for the above-mentioned contributions; but the pirates, to the intent that they should return speedily with those ransoms, tormented several cruelly in their presence, before they departed. After a few days, the Spaniards returned, telling Captain Morgan, 'We have ran up and down, and searched all the neighbouring woods and places we most suspected, and yet have not bean able to find any of our own party, nor consequently any fruit of our embassy; but if you are pleased to have a little longer patience with us, we shall certainly cause all that you demand to be paid within fifteen days;' which Captain Morgan granted. But not long after, there came into the town seven or eight pirates who had been ranging in the woods and fields, and got considerable booty. These brought amongst other prisoners, a negro, whom they had taken with letters. Captain Morgan having perused them, found that they were from the governor of Santa Jago, being written to some of the prisoners, wherein he told them, 'they should not make too much haste to pay any ransom for their town or persons, or any other pretext; but on the contrary, they should put off the pirates as well as they could with excuses and delays, expecting to be relieved by him in a short time, when he would certainly come to their aid.' Upon this intelligence Captain Morgan immediately ordered all their plunder to be carried aboard; and withal, he told the Spaniards, that the very next day they should pay their ransoms, for he would not wait a moment longer, but reduce the whole town to ashes, if they failed of the sum he demanded.

With this intimation, Captain Morgan made no mention to the Spaniards of the letters he had intercepted. They answered, 'that it was impossible for them to give such a sum of money in so short a space of time, seeing their fellow-townsmen were not to be found in all the country thereabouts.' Captain Morgan knew full well their intentions, but thought it not convenient to stay there any longer, demanding of them only five hundred oxen or cows, with sufficient salt to powder them, with this condition, that they should carry them on board his ships. Thus he departed with all his men, taking with him only six of the principal prisoners as pledges. Next day the Spaniards brought the cattle and salt to the ships, and required the prisoners; but Captain Morgan refused to deliver them, till they had helped his men to kill and salt the beeves: this was performed in great haste, he not caring to stay there any longer, lest he should be surprised by the forces that were gathering against him; and having received all on board his vessels, he set at liberty the hostages. Meanwhile there happened some dissensions between the English and the French: the occasion was as follows: A Frenchman being employed in killing and salting the beeves, an English pirate took away the marrow-bones he had taken out of the ox, which these people esteem much; hereupon they challenged one another: being come to the place of duel, the Englishman stabbed the Frenchman in the back, whereby he fell down dead. The other Frenchmen, desirous of revenge, made an insurrection against the English; but

Captain Morgan soon appeased them, by putting the criminal in chains to be carried to Jamaica, promising he would see justice done upon him; for though he might challenge his adversary, yet it was not lawful to kill him treacherously, as he did.

All things being ready, and on board, and the prisoners set at liberty, they sailed thence to a certain island, where Captain Morgan intended to make a dividend of what they had purchased in that voyage; where being arrived, they found nigh the value of fifty thousand pieces of eight in money and goods. The sum being known, it caused a general grief to see such a small purchase, not sufficient to pay their debts at Jamaica. Hereupon Captain Morgan proposed they should think on some other enterprise and pillage before they returned. But the French not being able to agree with the English, left Captain Morgan with those of his own nation, notwithstanding all the persuasions he used to reduce them to continue in his company. Thus they parted with all external signs of friendship.

The French went on to join the infamous l'Olonnais (Jean David Nau, a sailor from Sables d'Olonne in the Vendee, hence the name). l'Olonnais was a pirate without redeeming features. According to Exquemelin, 'After capturing Puerto Cavello, l'Olonnais and three hundred pirates headed for San Pedro where Spanish soldiers ambushed the buccaneers. Seeking a clear path into the city, l'Olonnais tortured the soldiers until they told him how to gain entry without encountering another ambush. He drew his cutlass, and with it cut open the breast of one of those poor

Spaniards, and pulling out his heart with his sacrilegious hands, began to bite and gnaw it with his teeth, like a ravenous wolf, saying to the rest: I will serve you all alike, if you show me not another way. L'Olonnais was a master torturer. Not only did he burn his victims or cut out their tongues, but when he began cutting them to pieces, he started with a slice of flesh, progressed to a hand, then an arm, and finally a leg. He favored the practice of "woolding," where he tied a cord around his victim's eyes and tightened the cord by twisting it with a stick until the man's eyes popped out of his head.' To an ordinary seaman, woolding is a method of serving rope with thinner stuff or even canvas bandage to protect it against chafe, and as an everyday activity turned to diabolical use must have been particularly horrifying for them. Perhaps the 'stick' Exquemelin refers to is a serving mallet. Morgan continued his marauding with his complement reduced by half. Exquemelin continues:

Captain Morgan, who knew very well all the avenues of this city and the neighbouring coasts, arrived in the dusk of the evening at Puerto de Naos, ten leagues to the west of Puerto Bello. Being come hither, they sailed up the river to another harbour called Puerto Pontin, where they anchored: here they put themselves into boats and canoes, leaving in the ships only a few men to bring them next day to the port. About midnight they came to a place called Esteralonga Lemos, where they all went on shore, and marched by land to the first posts of the city: they had in their company an Englishman, formerly a prisoner in those parts, who now served them for a guide: to him and three or four more they gave commission to take the sentinel, if possible, or kill him on the place: but they seized him so cunningly, as he had no time to give warning with his musket, or make any noise, and brought him, with his hands bound, to Captain Morgan, who asked him how things went in the city, and what forces they had; with other circumstances he desired to know. After every question they made him a thousand menaces to kill him, if he declared not the truth. Then they advanced to the city, carrying the said sentinel bound before them: having marched about a quarter of a league, they came to the castle near the city, which presently they closely surrounded, so that no person could get either in or out.

Being posted under the walls of the castle, Captain Morgan commanded the sentinel, whom they had taken prisoner, to speak to those within, charging them to surrender to his discretion; otherwise they should all be cut in pieces, without quarter. But they regarding none of these threats, began instantly to fire, which alarmed the city; yet notwithstanding, though the governor and soldiers of the said castle made as great resistance as could be, they were forced to surrender. Having taken the castle, they resolved to be as good as their words, putting the Spaniards to the sword, thereby to strike a terror into the rest of the city. Whereupon, having shut up all the soldiers and officers as prisoners into one room, they set fire to the powder (whereof they found great quantity) and blew up the castle into the air, with all the Spaniards that were within. This done, they pursued the course of their victory, falling upon the city, which, as yet, was not ready to receive them. Many of the inhabitants cast their precious jewels and money into wells and cisterns, or hid them in places underground, to avoid, as much as possible, being totally robbed. One of the party of pirates, assigned to this purpose, ran immediately to the cloisters, and took as many religious men and women as they could find. The governor of the city, not being able to rally the citizens, through their great confusion, retired to one of the castles remaining, and thence fired incessantly at the pirates: but these were not in the least negligent either to assault him, or defend themselves, so that amidst the horror of the assault, they made very few shots in vain; for aiming with great dexterity at the mouths of the guns, the Spaniards were certain to lose one or two men every time they charged each gun anew. This continued very furious from break of day till noon; yea, about this time of the day the case was very dubious which party should conquer, or be conquered. At last, the pirates perceiving they had lost many men, and yet advanced but little towards gaining either this, or the other castles, made use of fire-balls, which they threw with their hands, designing to burn the doors of the castles; but the Spaniards from the walls let fall great quantities of stones, and earthen pots full of powder, and other combustible matter, which forced them to desist. Captain Morgan seeing this generous defence made by the Spaniards, began to despair of success. Hereupon, many faint and calm meditations came into his mind; neither could he determine which way to turn himself in that strait. Being thus puzzled, he was suddenly animated to continue the assault, by seeing English colours put forth at one of the lesser castles, then entered by his men;

of whom he presently after spied a troop coming to meet him, proclaiming victory with loud shouts of joy. This instantly put him on new resolutions of taking the rest of the castles, especially seeing the chiefest citizens were fled to them, and had conveyed thither great part of their riches, with all the plate belonging to the churches and divine service.

To this effect, he ordered ten or twelve ladders to be made in all haste, so broad, that three or four men at once might ascend them: these being finished, he commanded all the religious men and women, whom he had taken prisoners, to fix them against the walls of the castle. This he had before threatened the governor to do, if he delivered not the castle: but his answer was, 'he would never surrender himself alive.' Captain Morgan was persuaded the governor would not employ his utmost force, seeing the religious women, and ecclesiastical persons, exposed in the front of the soldiers to the greatest danger. Thus the ladders, as I have said, were put into the hands of religious persons of both sexes, and these were forced, at the head of the companies, to raise and apply them to the walls: but Captain Morgan was fully deceived in his judgment of this design; for the governor, who acted like a brave soldier in performance of his duty, used his utmost endeavour to destroy whosoever came near the walls. The religious men and women ceased not to cry to him, and beg of him, by all the saints of heaven, to deliver the castle, and spare both his and their own lives; but nothing could prevail with his obstinacy and fierceness. Thus many of the religious men and nuns were killed before they could fix the ladders; which at last being done, though with great loss of the said religious people, the pirates mounted them in great numbers, and with not less valour, having fire-balls in their hands, and earthen pots full of powder; all which things, being now at the top of the walls, they kindled and cast in among the Spaniards.

This effort of the pirates was very great, insomuch that the Spaniards could no longer resist nor defend the castle, which was now entered. Hereupon they all threw down their arms, and craved quarter for their lives; only the governor of the city would crave no mercy, but killed many of the pirates with his own hands, and not a few of his own soldiers; because they did not stand to their arms. And though the pirates asked him if he would have quarter; yet he constantly answered, 'By no means, I had rather die as a valiant soldier, than be hanged as a coward.' They endeavoured as much as they could to take him prisoner, but he defended himself so obstinately, that they were forced to kill him, notwithstanding all the cries and tears of his own wife and daughter, who begged him, on their knees, to demand quarter, and save his life. When the pirates had possessed themselves of the castle, which was about night, they enclosed therein all the prisoners, placing the women and men by themselves, with some guards: the wounded were put in an apartment by itself, that their own complaints might be the cure of their diseases; for no other was afforded them.

This done, they fell to eating and drinking, as usual; that is, committing in both all manner of debauchery and excess, so that fifty courageous men might easily have retaken the city, and killed all the pirates. Next day, having plundered all they could find, they examined some of the prisoners (who had been persuaded by their companions to say they were the richest of the town), charging them severely to discover where they had hid their riches and goods. Not being able to extort anything from them, they not being the right persons, it was resolved to torture them: this they did so cruelly, that many of them died on the rack, or presently after. Now the president of Panama being advertised of the pillage and ruin of Puerto Bello, he employed all his care and industry to raise forces to pursue and cast out the pirates thence; but these cared little for his preparations, having their ships at hand, and determining to fire the city, and retreat. They had now been at Puerto Bello fifteen days, in which time they had lost many of their men, both by the unhealthiness of the country, and their extravagant debaucheries.

Hereupon, they prepared to depart, carrying on board all the pillage they had got, having first provided the fleet with sufficient victuals for the voyage. While these things were doing, Captain Morgan demanded of the prisoners a ransom for the city, or else he would burn it down, and blow up all the castles; withal, he commanded them to send speedily two persons, to procure the sum, which was 100,000 pieces of eight. To this effect two men were sent to the president of Panama, who gave him an account of all. The president, having now a body of men ready, set forth towards Puerto Bello, to encounter the pirates before their retreat; but, they, hearing of his coming, instead of flying away, went out to meet him at a narrow passage, which he must pass: here they placed a hundred men, very well armed, which at the first encounter put to flight a good party of those of Panama. This obliged the president to retire for that time, not being yet in a posture of strength to proceed farther. Presently after, he sent a message to Captain Morgan, to tell him, 'that if he departed not suddenly with all his forces from Puerto Bello, he ought to expect no quarter for himself, nor his companions, when he should take them, as he hoped soon to do.' Captain Morgan, who feared not his threats, knowing he had a secure retreat in his ships, which were at hand, answered, 'he would not deliver the castles, before he had received the contribution money he had demanded; which if it were not paid down, he would certainly burn the whole city, and then leave it, demolishing beforehand the castles, and killing the prisoners.'

The governor of Panama perceived by this answer that no means would serve to mollify the hearts of the pirates, nor reduce them to reason: hereupon, he determined to leave them, as also those of the city whom he came to relieve, involved in the difficulties of making the best agreement they could. Thus in a few days more the miserable citizens gathered the contributions required, and brought 100,000 pieces of eight to the pirates for a ransom of their cruel captivity: but the president of Panama was much amazed to consider that four hundred men could take such a great city, with so many strong castles, especially having no ordnance, wherewith to raise batteries, and, what was more, knowing the citizens of Puerto Bello had always great repute of being good soldiers themselves, and who never wanted courage in their own defence. This astonishment was so great, as made him send to Captain Morgan, desiring some small pattern of those arms wherewith he had taken with much vigour so great a city. Captain Morgan received this messenger very kindly, and with great civility; and gave him a pistol, and a few small bullets, to carry back to the president his master; telling him, withal, 'he desired him to accept that slender pattern of the arms wherewith he had taken Puerto Bello, and keep them for a twelve-month; after which time he promised to come to Panama, and fetch them away.' The governor returned the present very soon to Captain Morgan, giving him thanks for the favour of lending him such weapons as he needed not; and, withal, sent him a ring of gold, with this message, 'that he desired him not to give himself the labour of coming to Panama, as he had done to Puerto Bello: for he did assure him, he should not speed so well here, as he had done there.'

After this, Captain Morgan (having provided his fleet with all necessaries, and taken with him the best guns of the castles, nailing up the rest) set sail from Puerto Bello with all his ships, and arriving in a few days at Cuba, he sought out a place wherein he might quickly make the dividend of their spoil. They found in ready money 250,000 pieces of eight, besides other merchandises; as cloth, linen, silks, &c. With this rich purchase they sailed thence to their common place of rendezvous, Jamaica. Being arrived, they passed here some time in all sorts of vices and debaucheries, according to their custom; spending very prodigally what others had gained with no small labour and toil.

These don't sound to me like the actions of a licensed privateer, but of a pirate, and Morgan is all too readily comparable to l'Olonnais. Racking and woolding (except the non-naval sense of woolding) are the province of torturers, not military sailors. Even Exquemelin, one of their number, refers to his fellows as pirates: 'the governor of Panama perceived by this answer that no means would serve to mollify the hearts of the pirates.' We can be confident Exquemelin made no mistake in his vocabulary.

We're not sure exactly when Morgan was born, but we know when and how he died. He was able to enjoy the fruits of his piracy on Panama and Cuba, travelled to England where he moved about freely despite a warrant for his and the Jamaica Governor Modyford's arrest, brought about by pressure from the Spanish. Eventually, after three years at liberty in England, mixing in the highest circles, Morgan profited when the British and the Spanish fell out again. Charles II knighted Morgan and promoted him to Lieutenant Governor of Jamaica. The signal to the Spanish couldn't have been clearer. We know about the end of the pirate's life from the pen of Sir Hans Sloane (later inventor of drinking chocolate, collector of all sorts of art and artefacts and president of the Royal Society) who was then medical advisor to Jamaica's governor. Sloane treated Morgan during the last few months of his life. Sloane found him yellow and swollen. It sounds as if Morgan had some form of liver failure. Perhaps the rum got to him, perhaps some slow-acting Panamanian parasite was paying him back for his cruelties in Porto Bello. On 25 August 1688 Morgan died in bed. Four years later, in the earthquake of 1692, Port Royal Jamaica, Morgan's base during his pirate years, cracked apart and fell into the sea.

4

THE GREATEST ACT OF PIRACY

Henry Avery (he used various *noms de guerre* but I will stick with Henry Avery) began his career as a pirate in 1694, though he had spent some years as a midshipman in the Royal Navy. If Avery was among their number, the Royal Navy midshipmen of the seventeenth century must have been a rum lot, not the young gentlemen at sea who thought it improper to aim a gun at an individual (as opposed to his ship) during battle, as was the case in the late Georgian Royal Navy. According to Johnson/Defoe, by the 1690s Avery had been a slaver off the West African coast and had volunteered for service on a privateer, the *Charles II* (under Captain Gibson) as mate. It is unclear whether this means master's mate (i.e. midshipman described otherwise) or first officer (captain's deputy). Whatever his role, Avery felt more was needed to satisfy his talents, so he took over the *Charles II* with elements of her crew, renaming her the *Fancy*. The coup seems to have been well planned. Perhaps successful pirates have a 'planning' characteristic just as unsuccessful ones undoubtedly have a 'poor planning' characteristic. Avery planned to take over the *Charles II/Fancy*, planned to cruise West Africa and planned his attack on ships returning east from the yearly pilgrimage to Arabia, the obligation which modern Muslims call the Haj. Avery and his men knew that the pilgrimage would happen and when it would happen. Avery fell in with a couple of small pirate sloops, too small to confront a large and well-armed merchantman alone, but forming a power-ful pirate fleet with the *Fancy*. Johnson/Defoe continues:

They steered towards the Arabian Coast; near the River Indus, the Man at the Mast-Head spied a Sail, upon which they gave Chace, and as they came nearer to her, they perceived her to be a tall Ship, and fancied she might be a Dutch East-India Man homeward bound; but she proved a better Prize; when they fired at her to bring too, she hoisted Mogul's Colours, and seemed to stand upon her Defence; Avery only canonaded at a Distance, and some of his Men began to suspect that he was not the Hero they took him for: However, the Sloops made Use of their Time, and coming one on the Bow, and the other on the Quarter, of the Ship, clapt her on Board, and enter'd her, upon which she immediately struck her Colours and yielded; she was one of the Great Mogul's own Ships, and there were in her several of the greatest Persons of his Court, among whom it was said was one of his Daughters, who were going on a Pilgrimage to Mecca, the Mahometans thinking themselves obliged once in their Lives to visit that Place, and they were carrying with them rich Offerings to present at the Shrine of Mahomet. It is known that the Eastern People travel with the utmost Magnificence, so that they had with them all their Slaves and Attendants, their rich Habits and Jewels, with Vessels of Gold and Silver, and great Sums of Money to defray the Charges of their Journey by Land; wherefore the Plunder got by this Prize, is not easily computed.

Having taken all the Treasure on Board their own Ships, and plundered their Prize of every Thing else they either wanted or liked, they let her go; she not being able to continue her Voyage, returned back: As soon as the News came to the Mogul, and he knew that they were English who had robbed them, he threatened loud, and talked of sending a mighty Army with Fire and Sword, to extirpate the English from all their Settlements on the Indian Coast. The East-India Company in England, were very much alarmed at it; however, by Degrees, they found Means to pacify him, by promising to do their Endeavours to take the Robbers, and deliver them into his Hands; however, the great Noise this Thing made in Europe, as well as India, was the Occasion of all these romantick Stories which were formed of Avery's Greatness.

In the meantime our successful Plunderers agreed to make the best of their Way back to Madagascar, intending to make that Place their Magazine or Repository for all their Treasure, and to build a small Fortification there, and leave a few Hands always ashore to look after it, and defend it from any Attempts of the Natives; but Avery put an End of this Project, and made it altogether unnecessary. As they were steering their

Course, as has been said, he sends a Boat on Board of each of the Sloops, desiring the Chief of them to come on Board of him, in order to hold a Council; they did so, and he told them he had something to propose to them for the common Good, which was to provide against Accidents; he bad them consider the Treasure they were possess'd of, would be sufficient for them all if they could secure it in some Place on Shore; therefore all they had to fear, was some Misfortune in the Voyage; he bad them consider the Consequences of being separated by bad Weather, in which Case, the Sloops, if either of them should fall in with any Ships of Force, must be either taken or sunk, and the Treasure on Board her lost to the rest, besides the common Accidents of the Sea; as for his Part he was so strong, he was able to make his Party good with any Ship they were like to meet in those Seas; that if he met with any Ship of such Strength, that he could not take her, he was safe from being taken, being so well mann'd; besides his Ship was a quick Sailor, and could carry Sail, when the Sloops could not, wherefore, he proposed to them, to put the Treasure on Board his Ship, to seal up each Chest with 3 Seals, whereof each was to keep one, and to appoint a Rendezvous, in Case of Separation.

Upon considering this Proposal, it appeared so reasonable to them, that they readily came into it, for they argued to themselves, that an Accident might happen to one of the Sloops and the other escape, wherefore it was for the common Good. The Thing was done as agreed to, the Treasure put on Board of Avery, and the Chests seal'd; they kept Company that Day and the next, the Weather being fair, in which Time Avery tampered with his Men, telling them they now had sufficient to make them all easy, and what should hinder them from going to some Country, where they were not known, and living on Shore all the rest of their Days in Plenty; they understood what he meant: And in short, they all agreed to bilk their new Allies, the Sloop's Men, nor do I find that any of them felt any Qualms of Honour rising in his Stomach, to hinder them from consenting to this Piece of Treachery. In fine, they took Advantage of the Darkness that Night, steer'd another Course, and, by Morning, lost Sight of them. I leave the Reader to judge, what Swearing and Confusion there was among the Sloop's Men, in the Morning, when they saw that Avery had given them the Slip; for they knew by the Fairness of the Weather, and the Course they had agreed to steer, that it must have been done on purpose: But we leave them at present to follow Mr. Avery.

Avery, and his Men, having consulted what to do with themselves, came to a Resolution, to make the best of their Way towards America; and none of them being known in those Parts, they intended to divide the Treasure, to change their Names, to go ashore, some in one Place, some in other, to purchase some Settlements, and live at Ease. The first Land they made, was the Island of Providence, then newly settled; here they staid some Time, and having considered that when they should go to New-England, the Greatness of their Ship, would cause much Enquiry about them; and possibly some People from England, who had heard the Story of a Ship's being run away with from the Groine, might suspect them to be the People; they therefore took a Resolution of disposing of their Ship at Providence:

Upon which, Avery pretending that the Ship being fitted out upon the privateering Account, and having had no Success, he had received Orders from the Owners, to dispose of her to the best Advantage, he soon met with a Purchaser, and immediately bought a Sloop.

In this Sloop, he and his Companions embarq'd, they touch'd at several Parts of America, where no Person suspected them; and some of them went on Shore, and dispersed themselves about the Country, having received such Dividends as Avery would give them; for he concealed the greatest Part of the Diamonds from them, which in the first Hurry of plundering the Ship, they did not much regard, as not knowing their Value.

At length he came to Boston, in New-England, and seem'd to have a Desire of settling in those Parts, and some of his Companions went on Shore there also, but he changed his Resolution, and proposed to the few of his Companions who were left, to sail for Ireland, which they consented to: He found out that New-England was not a proper Place for him, because a great deal of his Wealth lay in Diamonds; and should he have produced them there, he would have certainly been seiz'd on Suspicion of Pyracy.

In their Voyage to Ireland, they avoided St. George's Channel, and sailing North about, they put into one of the Northern Ports of that Kingdom; there they disposed of their Sloop, and coming on Shore they separated themselves, some going to Cork, and some to Dublin, 18 of whom obtain'd their Pardons afterwards of K. William. When Avery had remain'd some Time in this Kingdom, he was afraid to offer his Diamonds to sale, least an Enquiry into his Manner of coming by them should occasion a Discovery; therefore considering with himself what was best to be done, he fancied there were some Persons at Bristol, whom he might venture to trust; upon which, he resolved to pass over into England; he did so, and going into Devonshire, he sent to one of these Friends to meet him at a Town called Biddiford; when he had communicated himself to his Friends, and consulted with him about the Means of his Effects, they agreed, that the safest Method would be, to put them in the Hands of some Merchants, who being Men of Wealth and Credit in the World, no Enquiry would be made how they came by them; this Friend telling him he was very intimate with some who were very fit for the Purpose, and if he would but allow them a good Commission would do the Business very faithfully.

Avery liked the Proposal, for he found no other Way of managing his Affairs, since he could not appear in them himself; therefore his Friend going back to Bristol, and opening the Matter to the Merchants, they made Avery a Visit at Biddiford, where, after some Protestations of Honour and Integrity, he delivered them his Effects, consisting of Diamonds and some Vessels of Gold; they gave him a little Money for his present Subsistance, and so they parted.

He changed his Name and lived at Biddiford, without making any Figure, and therefore there was no great Notice taken of him; yet let one or two of his Relations know where he was, who came to see him. In some Time his little Money was spent, yet he heard nothing from his Merchants; he writ to them often, and after much Importunity they sent him a small Supply, but scarce sufficient to pay his Debts: In fine, the Supplies they sent him from Time to Time, were so small, that they were not sufficient to give him Bread, nor could he get that little, without a great deal of Trouble and Importunity, wherefore being weary of his Life, he went privately to Bristol, to speak to the Merchants himself, where instead of Money he met a most shocking Repulse, for when he desired them to come to an Account with him, they silenced him by threatening to discover him, so that our Merchants were as good Pyrates at Land as he was at Sea.

Whether he was frightened by these Menaces, or had seen some Body else he thought knew him, is not known; but he went immediately over to Ireland, and from thence sollicited his Merchants very hard for a Supply, but to no Purpose, for he was even reduced to beggary: In this Extremity he was resolved to return and cast himself upon them, let the Consequence be what it would. He put himself on Board a trading Vessel, and work'd his Passage over to Plymouth, from whence he travelled on Foot to Biddiford, where he had been but a few Days before he fell sick and died; not being worth as much as would buy him a Coffin.

So ends the short, happy career of Henry Avery. By any standard he was successful in his piracy, though it didn't seem to do him any good. Bideford isn't St James's or Westminster, and frittering away his time unable to either spend or perhaps access his gold must have frustrated Avery. The Mughal was so angered at the loss of his treasure he wouldn't deal with the British East India Company, which was unsustainable for the British government. This meant Avery and his men were outlaws throughout the English-speaking world. No wonder Avery's merchant 'friends' in England were able to rook him without fear of reprisal. Avery suffered from the scale of his own success and, though apparently rich beyond compare, was unable to avail himself of the cash. Some things in his story are a bit odd. Why, for example, didn't he pass on most of his cash to the merchants but keep

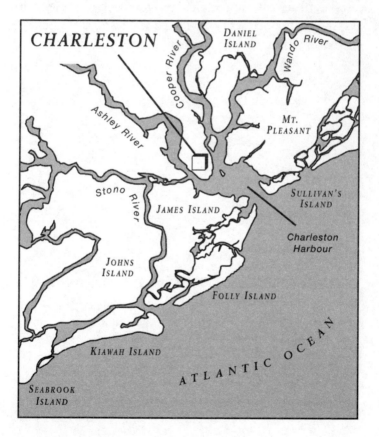

enough to support himself? Why allow himself to be reduced to beggary? It is as if the scale of Avery's success surprised and undid him and his original ability to plan deserted him. Perhaps he underwent a character change in Ireland and Bideford. Johnson/Defoe hints that, once removed from the sea, Morgan simply drank himself to death. Perhaps some similar fault underlies Avery. It's certainly true that, unlike most pirates, both of these men died in bed, but neither lasted long once the days of pirating were over. So much for successful pirates.

5

BLACKBEARD

Edward Teach, Blackbeard, is, of course, an archipirate. His behaviour is strongly reminiscent of l'Olonnais. However, he is such an enormous and semi-legendary figure in the history of piracy that he deserves a chapter of his own. Edward Teach, Blackbeard, is the man who most typifies what we think of as a pirate. His iconic image has certainly been exploited by Hollywood, by books and magazines and, of course, by Disney. The pirate in a tricorn hat with smouldering fuses in his hair and beard, cross belts laden with guns and cutlasses – that's Teach. He went out of his way to terrify his victims through his appearance and that of his crew, so that their submission would come all the easier. Teach isn't, of course, the first soldier or sailor to have discovered this psychological effect. Boarding parties from British men of war as late as the 1790s wore black scarves tied about their heads and made themselves up to look as fierce as possible. What a dispiriting sight 50 men wearing black scarves and bearing cutlasses must have made for their enemies, just as the devilish Teach, stepping on board a lightly armed merchantman through a cloud of gun-smoke, flashing cutlass in one hand and pistol in the other, black beard oiled, black eyes gleaming, fuses burning in both the hair and the beard, must have looked like Old Nick himself, supported by all his dark angels. If you were just an ordinary seaman with no interest in the ship above your wages, it wouldn't be very tempting to fight this devil for a share in the gold in the hold. Putting that thought in his victims' mind was exactly Teach's purpose. No wonder Teach was a success while he lasted. Edward Teach was born in approximately 1680, that is, 45 years after Morgan. He is known to have served in the War of the Spanish Succession, one of the scuffles over the influence of the Bourbon and Habsburg families which broke out in Europe from time to time. It's thought possibly 400,000 people died in this 'scuffle', which spread to the Spanish Main and the Americas. In other words, Teach himself steps out of a greater chaos to create one of his own. If piracy has a rule, this is it. John Milton's admonition to Fairfax comes to mind again, 'For what can war, but endless war, still breed?' Morgan and later Teach, seems to be the answer. Of Teach Captain Johnson tells us . . .

Edward Teach was a Bristol Man born, but had sailed some Time out of Jamaica in Privateers, in the late French War;[11] yet tho' he had often distinguished himself for his uncommon Boldness and personal Courage, he was never raised to any Command, till he went a-pyrating, which I think was at the latter End of the Year 1716,[12] when Captain Benjamin Hornigold put him into a Sloop that he had made Prize of, and with whom he continued in Consortship till a little while before Hornigold surrendered. In the Spring of the Year 1717, Teach and Hornigold sailed from Providence, for the Main of America, and took in their Way a Billop from the Havana, with 120 Barrels of Flower, as also a Sloop from Bermuda, Thurbar Master, from whom they took only some Gallons of Wine, and then let him go; and a Ship from Madera to South-Carolina, out of which they got Plunder to a considerable Value.

After cleaning on the Coast of Virginia, they returned to the West-Indies, and in the Latitude of 24, made Prize of a large French Guiney Man, bound to Martinico, which by Hornigold's Consent, Teach went aboard of as Captain, and took a Cruize in her; Hornigold returned with his Sloop to Providence, where, at the Arrival of Captain Rogers, the Governor, he surrendered to Mercy, pursuant to the King's Proclamation.

Aboard of this Guiney Man Teach mounted 40 Guns, and named her the Queen Ann's Revenge; and cruising near the Island of St. Vincent, took a large Ship, called the Great Allen, Christopher Taylor Commander; the Pyrates plundered her of what they thought fit, put all the Men ashore upon the Island above mentioned, and then set Fire to the Ship.

A few Days after, Teach fell in with the Scarborough Man of War, of 30 Guns, who engaged him for some Hours; but she finding the Pyrate well mann'd, and having tried her strength, gave over the Engagement, and returned to Barbadoes, the Place of her Station; and

Teach sailed towards the Spanish America. In his Way he met with a Pyrate Sloop of ten Guns, commanded by one Major Bonnet, lately a Gentleman of good Reputation and Estate in the Island of Barbadoes, whom he joyned; but in a few Days after, Teach, finding that Bonnet knew nothing of a maritime Life, with the Consent of his own Men, put in another Captain, one Richards, to command Bonnet's Sloop, and took the Major on aboard his own Ship, telling him, that as he had not been used to the Fatigues and Care of such a Post, it would be better for him to decline it, and live easy and at his Pleasure, in such a Ship as his, where he should not be obliged to perform Duty, but follow his own Inclinations. At Turniff, ten Leagues short of the Bay of Honduras, the Pyrates took in fresh Water; and while they were at an Anchor there, they saw a Sloop coming in, whereupon, Richards in the Sloop called the Revenge, slipped his Cable, and run out to meet her; who upon seeing the black Flag hoisted, struck his Sail and came to, under the Stern of Teach the Commadore. She was called the Adventure, from Jamaica, David Harriot Master. They took him and his Men aboard the great Ship, and sent a Number of other Hands with Israel Hands, Master of Teach's Ship, to Man the Sloop for the pyratical Account.

The 9th of April, they weighed from Turniff, having lain there about a Week, and sailed to the Bay, where they found a Ship and four Sloops, three of the latter belonged to Jonathan Bernard, of Jamaica, and the other to Captain James; the Ship was of Boston, called the Protestant Cæsar, Captain Wyar Commander. Teach hoisted his Black Colours, and fired a Gun, upon which Captain Wyar and all his Men, left their Ship, and got ashore in their Boat. Teach's Quarter-Master, and eight of his Crew, took Possession of Wyar's Ship, and Richards secured all the Sloops, one of which they burnt out of spight to the Owner; the Protestant Cæsar they also burnt, after they had plundered her, because she belonged to Boston, where some Men had been hanged for Pyracy; and the three Sloops belonging to Bernard they let go.

From hence the Rovers sailed to Turkill, and then to the Grand Caimanes, a small Island about thirty Leagues to the Westward of Jamaica, where they took a small Turtler, and so to the Havana, and from thence to the Bahama Wrecks, and from the Bahama Wrecks, they sailed to Carolina, taking a Brigantine and two Sloops in their Way, where they lay off the Bar of Charles-Town for five or six Days. They took here a Ship as she was coming out, bound for London, commanded by Robert Clark, with some Passengers on Board for England; the next Day they took another Vessel coming out of Charles-Town, and also two Pinks coming into Charles-Town; likewise a Brigantine with 14 Negroes aboard; all which being done in the Face of the Town, struck a great Terror to the whole Province of Carolina, having just before been visited by Vane, another notorious Pyrate, that they abandoned themselves to Dispair, being in no Condition to resist their Force. They were eight Sail in the Harbour, ready for the Sea, but none dared to venture out, it being almost impossible to escape their Hands. The inward bound Vessels were under the same unhappy Dilemma, so that the Trade of this Place was totally interrupted: What made these Misfortunes heavier to them, was a long expensive War, the Colony had had with the Natives, which was but just ended when these Robbers infested them.

Teach detained all the Ships and Prisoners, and, being in want of Medicines, resolves to demand a Chest from the Government of the Province; accordingly Richards, the Captain of the Revenge Sloop, with two or three more Pyrates, were sent up along with Mr. Marks, one of the Prisoners, whom they had taken in Clark's Ship, and very insolently made their Demands, threatning, that if they did not send immediately the Chest of Medicines, and let the Pyrate-Ambassadors return, without offering any Violence to their Persons, they would murder all their Prisoners, send up their Heads to the Governor, and set the Ships they had taken on Fire. Whilst Mr. Marks was making Application to the Council, Richards, and the rest of the Pyrates, walk'd the Streets publickly, in the Sight of all People, who were fired with the utmost Indignation, looking upon them as Robbers and Murtherers, and particularly the Authors of their Wrongs and Oppressions, but durst not so much as think of executing their Revenge, for fear of bringing more Calamities upon themselves, and so they were forced to let the Villains pass with Impunity.

This is new. Now Teach was apparently at war with the state. In the past pirates had made treaties and negotiated with governments. They would do it again in the future, but none so brazenly as Teach, who had stationed his ships at the mouth of the river, five miles from Charleston, and now had his embassy walking the streets. Morgan had committed similar acts, but always with the fig leaf of a privateer's letter of marque or commission from Jamaica. Not only had Teach moved quickly from the position of 'outlaw' to that of one confronting his own native state (America in 1717 was still British), he did so without, apparently, the slightest fear of retribution. Perhaps he'd just spotted a weak government in the Carolinas and was exploiting the weakness, but it was only months since Hornigold had submitted to British mercy.

The Government were not long in deliberating upon the Message, tho' 'twas the greatest Affront that could have been put upon them; yet for the saving so many Mens Lives, (among them, Mr. Samuel Wragg, one of the Council) they comply'd with the Necessity, and sent aboard a Chest, valued at between 3 and 400 l. and the Pyrates went back safe to their Ships.

Blackbeard, (for so Teach was generally called, as we shall hereafter shew) as soon as he had received the Medicines and his Brother Rogues, let go the Ships and the Prisoners; having first taken out of them in Gold and Silver, about 1500 l. Sterling, besides Provisions and other Matters. From the Bar of Charles-Town, they sailed to North-Carolina; Captain Teach in the Ship, which they called the Man of War, Captain Richards and Captain Hands in the Sloops, which they termed Privateers, and another Sloop serving them as a Tender. Teach began now to think of breaking up the Company, and securing the Money and the best of the Effects for himself, and some others of his Companions he had most Friendship for, and to cheat the rest: Accordingly, on Pretence of running into Topsail Inlet to clean, he grounded his Ship, and then, as if it had been done undesignedly, and by Accident; he orders Hands's Sloop to come to his Assistance, and get him off again, which he endeavouring to do, ran the Sloop on Shore near the other, and so were both lost. This done, Teach goes into the Tender Sloop, with forty Hands, and leaves the Revenge there; then takes seventeen others and Marroons them upon a small sandy Island, about a League from the Main, where there was neither Bird, Beast or Herb for their Subsistance, and where they must have perished if Major Bonnet had not two Days after taken them off.

Teach goes up to the Governor of North-Carolina with about twenty of his Men, surrender to his Majesty's Proclamation, and receive Certificates thereof, from his Excellency; but it did not appear that their submitting to this Pardon was from any Reformation of Manners, but only to wait a more favourable Opportunity to play the same Game over again; which he soon after effected, with greater Security to himself, and with much better Prospect of Success, having in this Time cultivated a very good understanding with Charles Eden, Esq; the Governor above mentioned.

This means Eden was corrupt. It was common enough. When Avery scored his improbable success by robbing the ships of the Great Mughal, his first real attempt at refuge was with a corrupt colonial governor. Thirty years later Teach was carrying out the same stunt.

The first Piece of Service this kind Governor did to Black-Beard was to give him a Right to the Vessel which he had taken, when he was a pyrating in the great Ship called the Queen Ann's Revenge; for which purpose, a Court of Vice-Admiralty was held at Bath-Town; and, tho' Teach had never any Commission in his Life, and the Sloop belonging to the English Merchants, and taken in Time of Peace; yet was she condemned as a Prize taken from the Spaniards, by the said Teach. These Proceedings shew that Governors are but Men.

Before he sailed upon his Adventures, he marry'd a young Creature of about sixteen Years of Age, the Governor performing the Ceremony. As it is a Custom to marry here by a Priest, so it is there by a Magistrate; and this, I have been informed, made Teach's fourteenth Wife, whereof, about a dozen might be still living. His Behaviour in this State, was something extraordinary; for while his Sloop lay in Okerecock Inlet, and he ashore at a Plantation, where his Wife lived, with whom after he had lain all Night, it was his Custom to invite five or six of his brutal Companions to come ashore, and he would force her to prostitute her self to them all, one after another, before his Face.

Little human behaviour is without meaning – some psychologists would say 'none' – and one has to wonder what exactly Teach was seeking here. Presumably Teach's sexual brutalization of his wife completed his 'outsider-ness'. Now no state, no convention, no religion, no man and no woman could inhibit his behaviour. He was a man who could do anything – at least as long as he remained at liberty. There may be another side to this sexual use of his wife or prostitution of her, as Defoe/Johnson calls it. It may be a form of the ceremonial male bonding beloved of armies, university fraternity societies and biker gangs.

In June 1718, he went to Sea, upon another Expedition, and steered his Course towards Bermudas; he met with two or three English Vessels in his Way, but robbed them only of Provisions, Stores and other Necessaries, for his present Expence; but near the Island aforementioned, he fell in with two French Ships, one of them was loaden with Sugar and Cocoa, and the other light, both bound to Martinico; the Ship that had no Lading he let go, and putting all the Men of the loaded Ship aboard her, he brought home the other with her Cargo to North-Carolina, where the Governor and the Pyrates shared the Plunder.

When Teach and his Prize arrived, he and four of his Crew went to his Excellency, and made Affidavit, that they found the French Ship at Sea, without a Soul on Board her; and then a Court was called, and the Ship condemned: The Governor had sixty Hogsheads of Sugar for his Dividend, and one Mr. Knight, who was his Secretary, and Collector for the Province, twenty, and the rest was shared among the other Pyrates.

The Business was not yet done, the Ship remained, and it was possible one or other might come into the River, that might be acquainted with her, and so discover the Roguery; but Teach thought of a Contrivance to prevent this, for, upon a Pretence that she was leaky, and that she might sink, and so stop up the Mouth of the Inlet or Cove where she lay, he obtained an Order from the Governor, to bring her out into the River, and set her on Fire, which was accordingly executed, and she was burnt down to the Water's Edge, her Bottom sunk, and with it, their Fears of her ever rising in Judgment against them. Captain Teach, alias Black-beard, passed three or four Months in the River, sometimes lying at Anchor in the Coves, at other Times sailing from one Inlet to another, trading with such Sloops as he met, for the Plunder he had taken, and would often give them Presents for Stores and Provisions took from them; that is, when he happened to be in a giving Humour; at other Times he made bold with them, and took what he liked, without saying, by your Leave, knowing well, they dared not send him a Bill for the Payment. He often diverted himself with going ashore among the Planters, where he revelled Night and Day: By these he was well received, but whether out of Love or Fear, I cannot say; sometimes he used them courteously enough, and made them Presents of Rum and Sugar, in Recompence of what he took from them; but, as for Liberties (which 'tis said) he and his Companions often took with the Wives and Daughters of the Planters, I cannot take upon me to say, whether he paid them ad Valorem, or no. At other Times he carried it in a lordly Manner towards them, and would lay some of them under Contribution; nay, he often proceeded to bully the Governor, not, that I can discover the least Cause of Quarrel betwixt them, but it seemed only to be done, to shew he dared do it.

The Sloops trading up and down this River, being so frequently pillaged by Black-beard, consulted with the Traders, and some of the best of the Planters, what Course to take; they saw plainly it would be in vain to make any Application to the Governor of North-Carolina, to whom it properly belonged to find some

Redress; so that if they could not be relieved from some other Quarter Black-beard would be like to reign with Impunity. Therefore, with as much Secrecy as possible, they sent a Deputation to Virginia, to lay the Affair before the Governor of that Colony, and to solicit an armed Force from the Men of War lying there, to take or destroy this Pyrate.

This Governor consulted with the Captains of the two Men of War, viz. the Pearl and Lime, who had lain in St. James's River, about ten Months. It was agreed that the Governor should hire a couple of small Sloops, and the Men of War should Man them; this was accordingly done, and the Command of them given to Mr. Robert Maynard, first Lieutenant of the Pearl, an experienced Officer, and a Gentleman of great Bravery and Resolution, as will appear by his gallant Behaviour in this Expedition. The Sloops were well mann'd and furnished with Ammunition and small Arms, but had no Guns mounted.

About the Time of their going out, the Governor called an Assembly, in which it was resolved to publish a Proclamation, offering certain Rewards to any Person or Persons, who, within a Year after that Time, should take or destroy any Pyrate: The original Proclamation being in our Hands, is as follows:

By his Majesty's Lieutenant Governor, and Commander in Chief, of the Colony and Dominion of Virginia,

A PROCLAMATION; Publishing the Rewards given for apprehending, or killing, Pyrates. Whereas, by an Act of Assembly, made at a Session of Assembly, begun at the Capital in Williamsburgh, the eleventh Day of

November, in the fifth Year of his Majesty's Reign, entituled, An Act to encourage the apprehending and destroying of Pyrates: It is, amongst other Things enacted, that all and every Person, or Persons, who, from and after the fourteenth Day of November, in the Year of our Lord one thousand seven hundred and eighteen, and before the fourteenth Day of November, which shall be in the Year of our Lord one thousand seven hundred and nineteen, shall take any Pyrate, or Pyrates, on the Sea or Land, or in Case of Resistance, shall kill any such Pyrate, or Pyrates, between the Degrees of thirty four, and thirty nine, of Northern Latitude, and within one hundred Leagues of the Continent of Virginia, or within the Provinces of Virginia, or North Carolina, upon the Conviction, or making due Proof of the killing of all, and every such Pyrate, and Pyrates, before the Governor and Council, shall be entitled to have, and receive out of the publick Money, in the Hands of the Treasurer of this Colony, the several Rewards following; that is to say, for Edward Teach, commonly call'd Captain Teach, or Black-Beard, one hundred Pounds, for every other Commander of a Pyrate Ship, Sloop, or Vessel, forty Pounds; for every Lieutenant, Master, or Quarter-Master, Boatswain, or Carpenter, twenty Pounds; for every other inferior Officer, fifteen Pounds, and for every private Man taken on Board such Ship, Sloop, or Vessel, ten Pounds; and, that for every Pyrate, which shall be taken by any Ship, Sloop or Vessel, belonging to this Colony, or North-Carolina, within the Time aforesaid, in any Place whatsoever, the like Rewards shall be paid according to the Quality and Condition of such Pyrates. Wherefore, for the Encouragement of all such

Persons as shall be willing to serve his Majesty, and their Country, in so just and honourable an Undertaking, as the suppressing a Sort of People, who may be truly called Enemies to Mankind: I have thought fit, with the Advice and Consent of his Majesty's Council, to issue this Proclamation, hereby declaring, the said Rewards shall be punctually and justly paid, in current Money of Virginia, according to the Directions of the said Act. And, I do order and appoint this Proclamation, to be published by the Sheriffs, at their respective County-Houses, and by all Ministers and Readers, in the several Churches and Chappels, throughout this Colony. Given at our Council-Chamber at Williamsburgh, this 24th Day of November, 1718, in the fifth Year of his Majesty's Reign.

GOD SAVE THE KING. A. SPOTSWOOD.

The 17th of November, 1718, the Lieutenant sail'd from Kicquetan, in James River in Virginia, and, the 21st in the Evening, came to the Mouth of Okerecock Inlet, where he got Sight of the Pyrate. This Expedition was made with all imaginable Secrecy, and the Officer manag'd with all the Prudence that was necessary, stopping all Boats and Vessels he met with, in the River, from going up, and thereby preventing any Intelligence from reaching Black-Beard, and receiving at the same time an Account from them all, of the Place where the Pyrate was lurking; but notwithstanding this Caution, Black-beard had Information of the Design, from his Excellency of the Province; and his Secretary, Mr. Knight, wrote him a Letter, particularly concerning it, intimating, That he had sent him four of his Men, which were all he could meet with, in or about Town, and so bid him be upon his

Guard. These Men belonged to Black-beard, and were sent from Bath-Town to Okerecock Inlet, where the Sloop lay, which is about 20 Leagues.

Black-beard had heard several Reports, which happened not to be true, and so gave the less Credit to this, nor was he convinced till he saw the Sloops: Whereupon he put his Vessel in a Posture of Defence; he had no more than twenty five Men on Board, tho' he gave out to all the Vessels he spoke with, that he had 40. When he had prepared for Battle, he set down and spent the Night in drinking with the Master of a trading Sloop, who, 'twas thought, had more Business with Teach, than he should have had.

Lieutenant Maynard came to an Anchor, for the Place being shoal, and the Channel intricate, there was no getting in, where Teach lay, that Night; but in the Morning he weighed, and sent his Boat a-head of the Sloops to sound; and coming within Gun-Shot of the Pyrate, received his Fire; whereupon Maynard hoisted the King's Colours, and stood directly towards him, with the best Way that his Sails and Oars could make. Black-beard cut his Cable, and endeavoured to make a running Fight, keeping a continual Fire at his Enemies, with his Guns; Mr. Maynard not having any, kept a constant Fire with small Arms, while some of his Men laboured at their Oars. In a little Time Teach's Sloop ran a-ground, and Mr. Maynard's drawing more Water than that of the Pyrate, he could not come near him; so he anchored within half Gun-Shot of the Enemy, and, in order to lighten his Vessel, that he might run him aboard, the Lieutenant ordered all his Ballast to be thrown overboard, and all the Water to be staved, and then weigh'd and stood for him; upon which Black-beard hail'd him in this rude Manner: Damn you for Villains, who are you? And, from whence came you? The Lieutenant made him Answer, You may see by our Colours we are no Pyrates. Black-beard bid him send his Boat on Board, that he might see who he was; but Mr. Maynard reply'd thus; I cannot spare my Boat, but I will come aboard of you as soon as I can, with my Sloop. Upon this, Black-beard took a Glass of Liquor, and drank to him with these Words: Damnation seize my Soul if I give you Quarters, or take any from you. In Answer to which, Mr. Maynard told him, That he expected no Quarters from him, nor should he give him any. By this time Blackbeard's Sloop fleeted, as Mr. Maynard's Sloops were rowing towards him, which being not above a Foot high in the Waste, and consequently the Men all exposed, as they came near together, (there being hitherto little or no Execution done, on either Side) the Pyrate fired a Broadside, charged with all Manner of small Shot. A fatal Stroke to them! The Sloop the Lieutenant was in, having twenty Men killed and wounded, and the other Sloop nine: This could not be help'd, for there being no Wind, they were oblig'd to keep to their Oars, otherwise the Pyrate would have got away from him, which, it seems, the Lieutenant was resolute to prevent.

After this unlucky Blow, Black-beard's Sloop fell Broadside to the Shore; Mr. Maynard's other Sloop, which was called the Ranger, fell a-stern, being, for the present, disabled; so the Lieutenant finding his own Sloop had Way, and would soon be on Board of Teach, he ordered all his Men down, for fear of another Broadside, which must have been their Destruction, and the loss of their Expedition. Mr. Maynard was the only Person that kept the Deck, except the Man at the Helm, whom he directed to lye down snug, and the Men in the Hold were ordered to get their Pistols and their Swords ready for close fighting, and to come up at his Command; in order to which, two Ladders were placed in the Hatch-Way for the more Expedition. When the Lieutenant's Sloop boarded the other, Captain Teach's Men threw in several new fashioned sort of Grenadoes, viz. Case Bottles fill'd with Powder, and small Shot, Slugs, and Pieces of Lead or Iron, with a quick Match in the Mouth of it, which being lighted without Side, presently runs into the Bottle to the Powder, and as it is instantly thrown on Board, generally does great Execution, besides putting all the Crew into a Confusion; but by good Providence, they had not that Effect here; the Men being in the Hold, and Black-beard seeing few or no Hands aboard, told his Men, That they were all knock'd on the Head, except three or four; and therefore, says he, let's jump on Board, and cut them to Pieces. Whereupon, under the Smoak of one of the Bottles just mentioned, Black-beard enters with fourteen Men, over the Bows of Maynard's Sloop, and were not seen by him till the Air cleared; however, he just then gave a Signal to his Men, who all rose in an Instant, and attack'd the Pyrates with as much Bravery as ever was done upon such an Occasion: Black-beard and the Lieutenant fired the first Pistol at each other, by which the Pyrate received a Wound, and then engaged with Swords, till the Lieutenant's unluckily broke, and stepping back to cock a Pistol, Black-beard, with his Cutlash, was striking at that instant, that one of Maynard's Men gave him a terrible

Wound in the Neck and Throat, by which the Lieutenant came off with a small Cut over his Fingers. They were now closely and warmly engaged, the Lieutenant and twelve Men, against Black-beard and fourteen, till the Sea was tinctur'd with Blood round the Vessel; Black-beard received a Shot into his Body from the Pistol that Lieutenant Maynard discharg'd, yet he stood his Ground, and sought with great Fury, till he received five and twenty Wounds, and five of them by Shot. At length, as he was cocking another Pistol, having fired several before, he fell down dead; by which Time eight more out of the fourteen dropp'd, and all the rest, much wounded, jump'd over-board, and call'd out for Quarters, which was granted, tho' it was only prolonging their Lives for a few Days. The Sloop Ranger came up, and attack'd the Men that remain'd in Black-beard's Sloop, with equal Bravery, till they likewise cry'd for Quarters.

Here was an End of that couragious Brute, who might have pass'd in the World for a Heroe, had he been employ'd in a good Cause; his Destruction, which was of such Consequence to the Plantations, was entirely owing to the Conduct and Bravery of Lieutenant Maynard and his Men, who might have destroy'd him with much less Loss, had they had a Vessel with great Guns; but they were obliged to use small Vessels, because the Holes and Places he lurk'd in, would not admit of others of greater Draught; and it was no small Difficulty for this Gentleman to get to him, having grounded his Vessel, at least, a hundred times, in getting up the River, besides other Discouragements, enough to have turn'd back any Gentleman without Dishonour, who was less resolute and bold than this Lieutenant.

So Blackbeard met his match.

An American newspaper reported the event thus:

Maynard and Teach themselves begun the fight with their swords, Maynard making a thrust, the point of his sword against Teach's cartridge box, and bent it to the hilt. Teach broke the guard of it, and wounded Maynard's fingers but did not disable him, whereupon he jumped back and threw away his sword and fired his pistol, which wounded Teach. Demelt struck in between them with his sword and cut Teach's face pretty much; in the interim both companies engaged in Maynard's sloop. Later during the battle, while Teach was loading his pistol he finally died from blood loss.

Lieutenant Maynard should be numbered among the first rank of the Royal Navy's heroes (though in fairness the action is celebrated yearly by the crew of HMS *Ranger*). Maynard was a man of utter conviction and enormous courage who attacked the pirate crew with only small arms against cannon and continued the attack when other men might have withdrawn. He seems to have been oblivious to his own safety and completely impervious to the pirate's savage reputation. Maynard was not finished yet:

The Lieutenant caused Black-beard's Head to be severed from his Body, and hung up at the Boltsprit End, then he sailed to Bath-Town, to get Relief for his wounded Men. It must be observed, that in rummaging the Pyrate's Sloop, they found several Letters and written Papers, which discovered the Correspondence betwixt Governor Eden, the Secretary and Collector, and also some Traders at New-York, and Black-beard. It is likely he had Regard enough for his Friends, to have destroyed these Papers before the Action, in order to hinder them from falling into such Hands, where the Discovery would be of no Use, either to the Interest or Reputation of these fine Gentlemen, if it had not been his fixed Resolution to have blown up together, when he found no possibility of escaping.

When the Lieutenant came to Bath-Town, he made bold to seize in the Governor's Store-House, the sixty Hogsheads of Sugar, and from honest Mr. Knight, twenty; which it seems was their Dividend of the Plunder taken in the French Ship; the latter did not long survive this shameful Discovery, for being apprehensive that he might be called to an Account for these Trifles, fell sick with the Fright, and died in a few Days.

After the wounded Men were pretty well recover'd, the Lieutenant sailed back to the Men of War in James River, in Virginia, with Black-beard's Head still hanging at the Bolt-sprit End, and five-teen Prisoners, thirteen of whom were hanged. It appearing upon Tryal, that one of them, viz. Samuel Odell, was taken out of the trading Sloop, but the Night before the Engagement. This poor Fellow was a little unlucky at his first entering upon his new Trade, there appearing no less than 70 Wounds upon him after the Action, notwithstanding which, he lived, and was cured of them all. The other Person that escaped the Gallows, was one Israel Hands, the Master [presumably this means sailing master, the man who would handle a sailing ship under the command of pirate captain

Teach] of Black-beard's Sloop, and formerly Captain of the same, before the Queen Ann's Revenge was lost in Topsail Inlet.

The aforesaid Hands happened not to be in the Fight, but was taken afterwards ashore at Bath-Town, having been sometime before disabled by Black-beard, in one of his savage Humours, after the following Manner. One Night drinking in his Cabin with Hands, the Pilot, and another Man; Black-beard without any Provocation privately draws out a small Pair of Pistols, and cocks them under the Table, which being perceived by the Man, he withdrew and went upon Deck, leaving Hands, the Pilot, and the Captain together. When the Pistols were ready, blew out the Candle, and crossing his hands, discharged them at his Company; Hands, the Master, was shot thro' the Knee, and lam'd for Life; the other Pistol did no Execution. Being asked the meaning of this, he only answered, by damning them, that if he did not now and then kill one of them, they would forget who he was.

Hands being taken, was try'd and condemned, but just as he was about to be executed, a Ship arrives at Virginia with a Proclamation for prolonging the Time of his Majesty's Pardon, to such of the Pyrates as should surrender by a limited Time therein expressed: Notwithstanding the Sentence, Hands pleaded the Pardon, and was allowed the Benefit of it, and is alive at this Time in London, begging his Bread.

Now that we have given some Account of Teach's Life and Actions, it will not be amiss, that we speak of his Beard, since it did not a little contribute towards making his Name so terrible in those Parts.

Plutarch, and other grave Historians have taken Notice, that several great Men amongst the Romans, took their Sir-Names from certain odd Marks in their Countenances; as Cicero, from a Mark or Vetch on his Nose; so our Heroe, Captain Teach, assumed the Cognomen of Black-beard, from that large Quantity of Hair, which, like a frightful Meteor, covered his whole Face, and frightened America more than any Comet that has appeared there a long Time.

This Beard was black, which he suffered to grow of an extravagant Length; as to Breadth, it came up to his Eyes; he was accustomed to twist it with Ribbons, in small Tails, after the Manner of our Ramilies Wiggs, and turn them about his Ears: In Time of Action, he wore a Sling over his Shoulders, with three brace of Pistols, hanging in Holsters like Bandaliers; and stuck lighted Matches under his Hat, which appearing on each Side of his Face, his Eyes naturally looking fierce and wild, made him altogether such a Figure, that Imagination cannot form an Idea of a Fury, from Hell, to look more frightful.

If he had the look of a Fury, his Humours and Passions were suitable to it; we shall relate two or three more of his Extravagancies, which we omitted in the Body of his History, by which it will appear, to what a Pitch of Wickedness, human Nature may arrive, if its Passions are not checked.

In the Common wealth of Pyrates, he who goes the greatest Length of Wickedness, is looked upon with a kind of Envy amongst them, as a Person of a more extraordinary Gallantry, and is thereby entitled to be distinguished by some Post, and if such a one has but

Courage, he must certainly be a great Man. The Hero of whom we are writing, was thoroughly accomplished this Way, and some of his Frolicks of Wickedness, were so extravagant, as if he aimed at making his Men believe he was a Devil incarnate; for being one Day at Sea, and a little flushed with drink, Come, says he, let us make a Hell of our own, and try how long we can bear it; accordingly he, with two or three others, went down into the Hold, and closing up all the Hatches, filled several Pots full of Brimstone, and other combustible Matter, and set it on Fire, and so continued till they were almost suffocated, when some of the Men cried out for Air; at length he opened the Hatches, not a little pleased that he held out the longest.

The Night before he was killed, he set up and drank till the Morning, with some of his own Men, and the Master of a Merchant-Man, and having had Intelligence of the two Sloops coming to attack him, as has been before observed; one of his Men asked him, in Case any thing should happen to him in the Engagement with the Sloops, whether his Wife knew where he had buried his Money? He answered, That no Body but himself and the Devil, knew where it was, and the longest Liver should take all. Those of his Crew who were taken alive, told a Story which may appear a little incredible; however, we think it will not be fair to omit it, since we had it from their own Mouths. That once upon a Cruize, they found out that they had a Man on Board more than their Crew; such a one was seen several Days amongst them, sometimes below, and sometimes upon Deck, yet no Man in the Ship could give an Account who he was, or from whence he came; but that he disappeared a little before they were cast away in their great Ship, but, it seems, they verily believed it was the Devil.

One would think these Things should induce them to reform their Lives, but so many Reprobates together, encouraged and spirited one another up in their Wickedness, to which a continual Course of drinking did not a little contribute; for in Black-beard's Journal, which was taken, there were several Memorandums of the following Nature, found writ with his own Hand, Such a Day, Rum all out; Our Company somewhat sober; A damn'd Confusion amongst us! Rogues a plotting; great Talk of Separation; So I look'd sharp for a Prize; such a Day took one, with a great deal of Liquor on Board, so kept the Company hot, damned hot, then all Things went well again. Thus it was these Wretches passed their Lives, with very little Pleasure or Satisfaction, in the Possession of what they violently take away from others.

This last section, even though it seems to claim Teach had the Devil for a crewman, is interesting. I underline the claim that Johnson/Defoe had the story of Teach's demise from eyewitness members of his own crew. If it is so it means that the reports of their behaviour, which plumbed the depths, are accurate in a very literal sense. I presume Hands was one of the witnesses interviewed, since Johnson/Defoe is able to say what became of him on his return to England. He became a beggar. Beggars or not, the men who escaped Teach's clutches and subsequently those of the law, and who returned to pass their lives in England were extraordinary lucky.

6

WOMEN PIRATES

Whatever the misogynistic nature of Blackbeard's crew and other pirate bands, such as Vikings, there were women pirates (as opposed to 'sailors' wives' i.e. prostitutes) on pirate ships contemporary or near contemporary to Teach. There are references to women companions to pirates throughout the literature on piracy.

Before examining Rackham's confederates I want to go back in time and look at a much bigger alleged pirate, Grace or Grania O'Malley. (As there are many versions of her name, due to the process of anglicizing the Gaelic, for brevity I will refer to her as Grace O'Malley.) Unlike some of the literary Amazonian-type figures of female myth (like Charlotte deBerry, a seventeenth-century woman pirate who – despite her apparently historical background – appears in literature first in the nineteenth century) Grace O'Malley is the subject first and foremost of historical documents. The evidence for her existence, if not all her actions, is as good as the evidence for yours or mine.

Grace was born about 1530 and died in about 1603. This makes her a direct contemporary of Elizabeth I, which is handy, as one of the proofs for Grace's existence is a meeting with Elizabeth I. At Grace's birth the O'Malleys were a seafaring family which controlled a part of what is now County Mayo. This control wasn't merely political influence. The set-up (though it was changing during the Tudor period) was that sub-divisions of Ireland were run on a more or less feudal system by local chieftains, each owing fealty to some overlord but having a enormous degree of independence within that system. No one was the king, though the clan chiefs did recognize a 'Lord of Ireland'. Henry VIII, the nearest very powerful king, was 'Lord of Ireland'. In an admirable piece of Realpolitik in 1541, at a meeting attended by the Irish clan chiefs, Henry VIII had been declared King of Ireland. Power expressed in the form of religious attachment was at the base of this declaration. Ireland was Catholic and the Irish considered the Pope their natural leader. But the attraction of Protestantism to late mediaeval monarchs like Henry is that it allowed kings to replace the Pope in the societal authority structure. Once he was installed as king, power descended to the Irish Lords from God via Henry VIII, or so went the theory. But Henry was of course unwilling to merely be titular King of Ireland, which is what he would be while military and tax gathering power persisted among the clans. How could he live with Irish clan leaders who recognized the authority of the Pope in Rome, gathered their own taxes and kept their own armed bands? The O'Malleys even had a few hundred gallowglass, a group of ferocious

Scottish mercenaries they could call on to exercise their will. The Pope had excommunicated Henry in 1533. This is the background to the O'Malleys' and eventually Grace O'Malley's conflict with the English Crown.

The O'Malleys traded overseas and taxed vessels which came into their waters. Grace is considered to have taken part in this trade as a young woman. Grace married Donal O'Flaherty, heir apparent to the Connemara fiefdom, with whom she had three children. This powerful couple then controlled a great deal of the sea trade in the west of Ireland from their strong point at Bunowen Castle, on a promontory thrown far into the Atlantic from Galway. When Donal died Grace moved to Clare Island in Clew Bay, 30 miles north and deep in O'Malley territory. It was clearly safer. This move coincided with the beginning of complaints to Dublin about O'Malley 'taxes' being a form of piracy. O'Malley's ships would stop and board the traders and demand payment for safe passage the rest of the way to Galway. Is this piracy? It mustn't be forgotten that complaints about the O'Malleys began just at a time when the Tudors wanted to exert more direct control on Ireland and just at the time when they (the clans O'Malley and O'Flaherty) had a woman leader and might be considered weaker. There are legends and tales about O'Malley taking castles for all sorts of romantic reasons, but even if the truth of these activities hangs in the balance they need to be seen against a political backdrop. English Tudor power (by now in the form of Queen Elizabeth I's soldiers and officials) was flooding Ireland. In these circumstances the independent and autonomous 'Queen' Grace O'Malley with her own standing army and her own system of taxes wasn't only unwelcome but high on the list of feudal lords who should submit. Governments see the taxation of citizens and running of armies as their prerogative and the government of Ireland wasn't on Clare Island but in Dublin and controlled by England. The O'Malleys, led by Grace, found themselves now in direct competition with the English monarchy.

In 1593, two of O'Malley's sons were made prisoner by the English government. Grace took the extraordinary step of visiting England to petition Elizabeth direct. She met Elizabeth at Greenwich, surrounded by Elizabeth's court. This is the most extraordinary event (though not unique, for Elizabeth had the adventurer Raleigh as a favourite, and Charles II used Captain Morgan as an advisor; both had grabbed Spanish territories by main force and enriched themselves while doing so). One wonders to what extent the meeting was brought about by Elizabeth's interest in another powerful woman – there is no shortage of apocryphal or semi-apocryphal stories about daggers and hankies and conversation in Latin during the meeting. Undoubtedly there was a political motive to the meeting; it took place five years after the Spanish Armada during a period when Elizabeth would have preferred to find an order in Ireland which didn't make such enormous demands on the English purse. If Elizabeth could have easily subjugated Grace and the O'Malleys there would have been no reason for a meeting. To invite Grace to court then grant her wishes is nothing short of a charm offensive from the Faerie Queen Elizabeth. This implies that winning over Grace O'Malley would have been a huge diplomatic success for Elizabeth. In the short term Grace got her way. Her sons were freed and Elizabeth's representative in Ireland – Richard Bingham, who was particularly offensive to the O'Malleys and had at one time imprisoned Grace – was temporarily withdrawn. The letter Elizabeth sent to Bingham following her meeting still exists. In it she orders him to release Grace's family. However, if the meeting in Greenwich was meant to put an end to the Irish separatist struggle it failed. Eventually Grace and the O'Malleys returned to what the English saw as their piracy, and in the long run Elizabeth merely strengthened English military rule in Ireland with a savagery which was unmatched until Cromwell. Elizabeth and Grace O'Malley died within months of each other in 1603. Was O'Malley a 'Pirate Queen'? She's usually referred to as such, and there are definite piratical facets to her activities off the West Coast of Ireland. But she didn't roam the Thames or Hudson River or the Spanish Main looking for victims. Grace O'Malley operated on her home shore. At worst she was the leader of a band of West Coast Irish robbers, at best she was an Irish chieftain looking for ways to defend her ancestral lands from a foreign and Protestant crown and raising taxes from visiting ships to do so. Elizabeth herself must have been inclined to the latter view – she didn't entertain visitors at her court unless they would serve some political purpose. A simple pirate could be suppressed by naval force at the end of the sixteenth century much as at the end of the seventeenth century. Elizabeth was dealing with a different problem.

The two most famous women pirates are probably Anne Bonney and Mary Read. They were unequivocally pirates. They sailed on a pirate ship and were captured and tried as pirates. They both sailed with pirate captain John Rackham, commonly known as Calico Jack because of his penchant for the printed calico cotton cloth popular at the time for women's clothing. Rackham is another of those brief-career ne'er-do-wells who dot the history of piracy in the Spanish Main. He was an 'officer' on the *Ranger*, the ship of New Providence (i.e. Bahamas) pirate Charles Vane and was voted to replace Vane when the latter apparently lost his nerve when faced with a French warship. New Providence was a nest of pirates and the British government had sent a well-known privateer, Woodes Rogers, to act as governor and suppress the piratical activities in what was effectively a free port. Since Woodes Rogers was offering pirate amnesties, one might wonder if the real cause of the replacement of Vane was an argument over the direction the *Ranger* was taking. Rackham returned to New Providence soon after taking control of her. Politics is the same whether on land or sea. Rackham cast Vane adrift and took command of the *Ranger*. He attacked a couple more merchant ships and then returned to Nassau, where he met Anne Bonney in a tavern and managed to charm her away from her 'husband'. David Cordingly describes him thus in the *Dictionary of National Biography*: 'essentially a small-time and not particularly bloodthirsty pirate, who preyed mostly on fishing boats and small coastal vessels, his main claim to fame is that his ship was the one in which two female pirates, Anne Bonney and Mary Read, pursued their scandalous careers. Rackham was supposedly a tall, dark-eyed, handsome man whose swashbuckling manner was matched and supported by his theatrical dress: striped calico shirt, jacket, and trousers.' I can't improve on that. Of Bonney and Read Johnson/Defoe writes:

> Anne Bonney was born at a Town near Cork, in the Kingdom of Ireland, her Father an Attorney at Law, but Anne was not one of his legitimate Issue, which seems to cross an old Proverb, which says, that Bastards have the best Luck . . .

Anne's mother had been the maidservant and lover of a Cork lawyer. His jealous wife had accused her of the theft of spoons and the maidservant had been imprisoned. She was freed when she was found to be pregnant, then Anne's lawyer father found his wife was pregnant too, and after a series of disputes over money:

> . . . he thought of removing, and turning what Effects he had into ready Money; he goes to Cork, and there with his Maid and Daughter embarques for Carolina.

It could come straight out of a story by Defoe himself, or Ainsworth or Thackeray.

> At first he followed the Practice of the Law in that Province, but afterwards fell into Merchandize, which proved more successful to him, for he gained by it sufficient to purchase a considerable Plantation: His

Maid, who passed for his Wife, happened to dye, after which his Daughter, our Anne Bonney, now grown up, kept his House ... It was certain she was so robust, that once, when a young Fellow would have lain with her, against her Will, she beat him so, that he lay ill of it a considerable Time.

This spitfire fell in love with a sailor of whom her father didn't approve (who was he to complain, you may wonder) so the two married and set off for New Providence to seek their fortune. In the early years of the eighteenth century there was only one type of fortune to be found in Nassau and only one way of getting it. Anne and her new husband set out to be pirates. Johnson/Defoe continues:

Here she became acquainted with Rackam the Pyrate, who making Courtship to her, soon found Means of withdrawing her Affections from her Husband, so that she consented to elope from him, and go to Sea with Rackam in Men's Cloaths: She was as good as her Word, and after she had been at Sea some Time, she proved with Child, and beginning to grow big, Rackam landed her on the Island of Cuba; and recommending her there to some Friends of his, they took Care of her, till she was brought to Bed: When she was up and well again, he sent for her to bear him Company.

The King's Proclamation being out, for pardoning of Pyrates, he took the Benefit of it, and surrendered; afterwards being sent upon the privateering Account, [in other words, having been commissioned as a privateer by Woodes Rogers, the Bahamian Governor] he returned to his old Trade ... In all these Expeditions, Anne Bonney bore him Company, and when any Business was to be done in their Way, no Body was more forward or couragious than she, and particularly when they were taken; she and Mary Read, with one more, were all the Persons that durst keep the Deck, as has been before hinted.

We have the story of their capture a few lines later:

Her Father was known to a great many Gentlemen, Planters of Jamaica, who had dealt with him, and among whom he had a good Reputation; and some of them, who had been in Carolina, remember'd to have seen her in his House; wherefore they were inclined to shew her Favour, but the Action of leaving her Husband was an ugly Circumstance against her. The Day that Rackam was executed, by special Favour, he was admitted to see her; but all the Comfort she gave him, was, that she was sorry to see him there, but if he had fought like a Man, he need not have been hang'd like a Dog.

She was continued in Prison, to the Time of her lying in, and afterwards reprieved from Time to Time; but what is become of her since, we cannot tell; only this we know, that she was not executed.

Johnson may not know what happened to her, but we do. Her father secured her release, then Anne returned to the Carolinas and raised a family of her own, eight further children in all. Anne Bonney lived until the age of 84 – in other words, she lived in Charleston for ten years after the formation of the United States of America. Was the child born in prison a little Rackham? We'll never know. But the story of Mary Read fills in a considerable number of gaps in the pirate narrative of Bonney.

Johnson/Defoe writes:

Mary Read was born in England, her Mother was married young, to a Man who used the Sea, who going a Voyage soon after their Marriage, left her with Child, which Child proved to be a Boy. As to the Husband, whether he was cast away, or died in the Voyage, Mary Read could not tell; but however, he never returned more; nevertheless, the Mother, who was young and airy, met with an Accident, which has often happened to Women who are young, and do not take a great deal of Care; which was, she soon proved with Child again, without a Husband to Father it, but how, or by whom, none but her self could tell, for she carried a pretty good Reputation among her Neighbours. Finding her Burthen grow, in order to conceal her Shame, she takes a formal Leave of her Husband's Relations, giving out, that she went to live with some Friends of her own, in the Country: Accordingly she went away, and carried with her her young Son, at this Time, not a Year old: Soon after her Departure her Son died, but Providence in Return, was pleased to give her a Girl in his Room, of which she was safely delivered, in her Retreat, and this was our Mary Read.

Here the Mother liv'd three or four Years, till what Money she had was almost gone; then she thought of returning to London, and considering that her Husband's

Mother was in some Circumstances, she did not doubt but to prevail upon her, to provide for the Child, if she could but pass it upon her for the same, but the changing a Girl into a Boy, seem'd a difficult Piece of Work, and how to deceive an experienced old Woman, in such a Point, was altogether as impossible; however, she ventured to dress it up as a Boy, brought it to Town, and presented it to her Mother in Law, as her Husband's Son; the old Woman would have taken it, to have bred it up, but the Mother pretended it would break her Heart, to part with it; so it was agreed betwixt them, that the Child should live with the Mother, and the supposed Grandmother should allow a Crown a Week for it's Maintainance.

Thus the Mother gained her Point, she bred up her Daughter as a Boy, and when she grew up to some Sense, she thought proper to let her into the Secret of her Birth, to induce her to conceal her Sex. It happen'd that the Grandmother died, by which Means the Subsistance that came from that Quarter, ceased, and they were more and more reduced in their Circumstances; wherefore she was obliged to put her Daughter out, to wait on a French Lady, as a Foot-boy, being now thirteen Years of Age: Here she did not live long, for growing bold and strong, and having also a roving Mind, she entered her self on Board a Man of War, where she served some Time, then quitted it, went over into Flanders, and carried Arms in a Regiment of Foot, as a Cadet; and tho' upon all Actions, she behaved herself with a great deal of Bravery, yet she could not get a Commission, they being generally bought and sold; therefore she quitted the Service, and took on in a Regiment of Horse; she behaved so well in several Engagements, that she got the Esteem of all her Officers; but her Comrade who was a Fleming, happening to be a handsome young Fellow, she falls in Love with him, and from that Time, grew a little more negligent in her Duty, so that, it seems, Mars and Venus could not be served at the same Time; her Arms and Accoutrements which were always kept in the best Order, were quite neglected: 'tis true, when her Comrade was ordered out upon a Party, she used to go without being commanded, and frequently run herself into Danger, where she had no Business, only to be near him; the rest of the Troopers little suspecting the secret Cause which moved her to this Behaviour, fancied her to be mad, and her Comrade himself could not account for this strange Alteration in her, but Love is ingenious, and as they lay in the same Tent, and were constantly together, she found a Way of letting him discover her Sex, without appearing that it was done with Design. He was much surprized at what he found out, and not a little pleased, taking it for granted, that he should have a Mistress solely to himself, which is an unusual Thing in a Camp, since there is scarce one of those Campaign Ladies, that is ever true to a Troop or Company; so that he thought of nothing but gratifying his Passions with very little Ceremony; but he found himself strangely mistaken, for she proved very reserved and modest, and resisted all his Temptations, and at the same Time was so obliging and insinuating in her Carriage, that she quite changed his Purpose, so far from thinking of making her his Mistress, he now courted her for a Wife.

This was the utmost Wish of her Heart, in short, they exchanged Promises, and when the Campaign was over, and the Regiment marched into Winter Quarters, they bought Woman's Apparel for her, with such Money as they could make up betwixt them, and were publickly married.

The Story of two Troopers marrying each other, made a great Noise, so that several Officers were drawn by Curiosity to assist at the Ceremony, and they agreed among themselves that every one of them should make a small Present to the Bride, towards House-keeping, in Consideration of her having been their fellow Soldier. Thus being set up, they seemed to have a Desire of quitting the Service, and settling in the World; the Adventure of their Love and Marriage had gained them so much Favour, that they easily obtained their Discharge, and they immediately set up an Eating House or Ordinary, which was the Sign of the Three Horse-Shoes, near the Castle of Breda, where they soon run into a good Trade, a great many Officers eating with them constantly. But this Happiness lasted not long, for the Husband soon died, and the Peace of Reswick being concluded, there was no Resort of Officers to Breda, as usual; so that the Widow having little or no Trade, was forced to give up Housekeeping, and her Substance being by Degrees quite spent, she again assumes her Man's Apparel, and going into Holland, there takes on in a Regiment of Foot, quarter'd in one of the Frontier Towns: Here she did not remain long, there was no likelihood of Preferment in Time of Peace, therefore she took a Resolution of seeking her Fortune another Way; and withdrawing from the Regiment, ships herself on Board of a Vessel bound for the West-Indies.

There is quite a resemblance to Moll Flanders at this point, except that the husband had been a fellow trooper and not Read's brother (as is the case in the plot of *Moll Flanders*). Though Read's and Bonney's stories sound extraordinary, a cursory reading of the *Newgate Calendar* or http://oldbaileyonline.org/will reveal dozens of landlocked young women whose lives were the equivalent of being tossed about like a cork at sea, ambition thwarted by one tragedy or another, and all the time with the abyss of death, unwanted pregnancy (which brought great risk of death and certainty of further poverty), transportation or a death sentence for some small crime. The Americas must have seemed like a horizon with a gleaming free future to people like the Bonneys or Mary Read. The Carolina plantations are a very long way from an impoverished widowhood in Breda. Mary didn't even get across the Atlantic before the project went wrong.

> It happen'd this Ship was taken by English Pyrates, and Mary Read was the only English Person on Board, they kept her amongst them, and having plundered the Ship, let it go again; after following this Trade for some Time, the King's Proclamation came out, and was publish'd in all Parts of the West-Indies, for pardoning such Pyrates, who should voluntarily surrender themselves by a certain Day therein mentioned.

Note Mary has done nothing to reveal herself as a woman at this point. She has become a pirate with the others, has military skills and was no doubt a welcome member of the pirate crew. However, it is a bit odd and Blackadder-ish that no one noticed she was a woman.

The Crew of Mary Read took the Benefit of this Proclamation, and having surrender'd, liv'd quietly on Shore; but Money beginning to grow short, and hearing that Captain Woods Rogers, Governor of the Island of Providence, was fitting out some Privateers to cruise against the Spaniards, she with several others embark'd for that Island, in order to go upon the privateering Account, being resolved to make her Fortune one way or other.

This is of course where she met Rackham and Bonney, after Rackham had taken advantage of an amnesty given by George I through his governor, former privateer Woodes Rogers. Mary joined up with Rackham as a fully fledged privateer – and there was still no clue she was a woman.

These Privateers were no sooner sail'd out, but the Crews of some of them, who had been pardoned, rose against their Commanders, and turned themselves to their old Trade: In this Number was Mary Read. It is true, she often declared, that the Life of a Pyrate was what she always abhor'd, and went into it only upon Compulsion, both this Time, and before, intending to quit it, whenever a fair Opportunity should offer itself; yet some of the Evidence against her, upon her Tryal, who were forced Men, and had sailed with her, deposed upon Oath, that in Times of Action, no Person amongst them were more resolute, or ready to Board or undertake any Thing that was hazardous, as she and Anne Bonney; and particularly at the Time they were attack'd and taken, when they came to close Quarters, none kept the Deck except Mary Read and Anne Bonney, and one more; upon which, she, Mary Read, called to those under Deck, to come up and fight like Men, and they did not stir, fired her Arms down the Hold amongst them, killing one, and wounding others. This was part of the Evidence against her, which she denied; which, whether true or no, thus much is certain, that she did not want Bravery, nor indeed was she less remarkable for her Modesty, according to her Notions of Virtue: Her Sex was not so much as suspected by any Person on Board, till Anne Bonney, who was not altogether so reserved in point of Chastity, took a particular liking to her; in short, Anne Bonney took her for a handsome young Fellow, and for some Reasons best known to herself, first discovered her Sex to Mary Read; Mary Read knowing what she would be at, and being very sensible of her own Incapacity that Way, was forced to come to a right Understanding with her, and so to the great Disappointment of Anne Bonney, she let her know she was a Woman also; but this Intimacy so disturb'd Captain Rackam, who was the Lover and Gallant of Anne Bonney, that he grew furiously jealous, so that he told Anne Bonney, he would cut her new Lover's Throat, therefore, to quiet him, she let him into the Secret also.

Captain Rackam (as he was enjoined) kept the Thing a Secret from all the Ship's Company, yet, notwithstanding all her Cunning and Reserve, Love found her out in this Disguise, and hinder'd her from forgetting her Sex. In their Cruize they took a great Number of Ships belonging to Jamaica, and other Parts of the West-Indies, bound to and from England; and when ever they meet any good Artist, or other Person that might be of any great Use to their Company, if he was not willing to enter, it was their Custom to keep him by Force. Among these was a young Fellow of a most engageing Behaviour, or, at least, he was so in the Eyes of Mary Read, who became so smitten with his Person and Address, that she could neither rest, Night or Day; but as there is nothing more ingenious than Love, it was no hard Matter for her, who had before been practiced in these Wiles, to find a Way to let him discover her Sex: She first insinuated her self into his liking, by talking against the Life of a Pyrate, which he was altogether averse to, so they became Mess-Mates and strict Companions: When she found he had a Friendship for her, as a Man, she suffered the Discovery to be made, by carelesly shewing her Breasts, which were very White.

The young Fellow, who was made of Flesh and Blood, had his Curiosity and Desire so rais'd by this Sight, that he never ceased importuning her, till she confessed what she was. Now begins the Scene of Love; as he had a Liking and Esteem for her, under her supposed Character, it was now turn'd into Fondness and Desire; her Passion was no less violent than his, and perhaps she express'd it, by one of the most generous Actions that ever Love inspired. It happened this young Fellow had a Quarrel with one of the Pyrates, and their Ship then lying at an Anchor, near one of the Islands, they had appointed to go ashore and fight, according to the Custom of the Pyrates: Mary Read, was to the last Degree uneasy and anxious, for the Fate of her Lover; she would not have had him refuse the Challenge, because, she could not bear the Thoughts of his being branded with Cowardice; on the other Side, she dreaded the Event, and apprehended the Fellow might be too hard for him: When Love once enters into the Breast of one who has any Sparks of Generosity, it stirs the Heart up to the most noble Actions; in this Dilemma, she shew'd, that she fear'd more for his Life than she did for her own; for she took a Resolution of quarrelling with this Fellow her self, and having challenged him ashore, she appointed the Time two Hours sooner than that when he was to meet her Lover, where she fought him at Sword and Pistol, and killed him upon the Spot.

It is true, she had fought before, when she had been insulted by some of those Fellows, but now it was altogether in her Lover's Cause, she stood as it were betwixt him and Death, as if she could not live without him. If he had no regard for her before, this Action would have bound him to her for ever; but there was no Occasion for Ties or Obligations, his Inclination towards her was sufficient; in fine, they applied their Troth to each other, which Mary Read said, she look'd upon to be as good a Marriage, in Conscience, as if it had been done by a Minister in Church; and to this was owing her great Belly, which she pleaded to save her Life.

She declared she had never committed Adultery or Fornication with any Man, she commended the Justice of the Court, before which she was tried, for distinguishing the Nature of their Crimes; her Husband, as she call'd him, with several others, being acquitted; and being ask'd, who he was? she would not tell, but, said he was an honest Man, and had no Inclination to such Practices, and that they had both resolved to leave the Pyrates the first Opportunity, and apply themselves to some honest Livelyhood.

It is no doubt, but many had Compassion for her, yet the Court could not avoid finding her Guilty; for among other Things, one of the Evidences against her, deposed, that being taken by Rackam, and detain'd some Time on Board, he fell accidentally into Discourse with Mary Read, whom he taking for a young Man, ask'd her, what Pleasure she could have in being concerned in such Enterprizes, where her Life was continually in Danger, by Fire or Sword; and not only so, but she must be sure of dying an ignominious Death, if she should be taken alive? – She answer'd, that as to hanging, she thought it no great Hardship, for, were it not for that, every cowardly Fellow would turn Pyrate, and so infest the Seas, that Men of Courage must starve: – That if it was put to the Choice of the Pyrates, they would not have the punishment less than Death, the Fear of which, kept some dastardly Rogues honest; that many of those who are now cheating the Widows and Orphans, and oppressing their poor Neighbours, who have no Money to obtain Justice, would then rob at Sea, and the Ocean would be crowded with Rogues, like the Land, and no Merchant would venture out; so that the Trade, in a little Time, would not be worth following.

Being found quick with Child, as has been observed, her Execution was respited, and it is possible she would have found Favour,[13] but she was seiz'd with a violent Fever, soon after her Tryal, of which she died in Prison.

The pirates, including Read and Bonney, were tried in Spanish Town, Jamaica, found guilty and sentenced to death. Both were reprieved on account of pregnancy. So might end the story of Mary Read and Anne Bonney, both pregnant, both imprisoned in Jamaica, each headed, apparently, towards the same fate. What happened is that both found very different ends. The difference appears to have been money and political interest. Anne's father quickly secured her release from gaol into his custody. Mary Read died in prison and was buried in April 1722 in St Catherines. Perhaps Anne Bonney was just a little like Patti Hearst. Is there any real evidence that she and Mary lived in a *ménage à trois* with Rackham, as some authors claim? It seems unlikely. There's no hint of it in Johnson/Defoe or at their trial. And the two women don't seem to have had a very high opinion of Rackham, having seen him in action. Did Mary have a lesbian affair with Anne? It's quite possible, though again there is precious little sign of it, whereas Johnson/Defoe allows himself plenty of space to indicate that Anne Bonney was promiscuous and was surprised, when she took a fancy to Mary, to discover Mary was in fact a woman. Johnson/Defoe was writing a long time before Queen Victoria's famous declaration that such things (as homosexuality) aren't possible for women, and he is uninhibited when describing other sexual arrangements, such as, for example, Teach and his 'wives'. If Johnson/Defoe, who was their contemporary, really thought Anne and Mary were lovers I believe he would have said so. In any case, Anne didn't impregnate Mary, whereas Mary gives an account at her trial of her anonymous lover and her pregnancy and is subsequently held back from the gallows because of the pregnancy he caused. Why not believe her? Johnson/Defoe tells us Mary had a lover on board the ship who'd been taken from another ship. So this man became a 'pirate' in the same way as Mary had become one. As we saw earlier in the case of other crews accused of piracy, it wasn't always easy for authorities faced with a ship full of pirates and prisoners to sort out who was a volunteer pirate and who was forced. Presumably Mary felt that this lover, who had clearly escaped trial, would have been in danger of being ascribed the status of pirate, not victim, if he was known to have slept with her. Everything we know about Mary says she was brave and steadfast. She wouldn't give her lover away.

And what of Rackham? Johnson/Defoe writes that Rackham didn't reveal Mary as a woman on board the ship. Why? Maybe it would have been more trouble than it was worth – he'd have half the crew fighting over her. Maybe he was afraid of these two powerful and apparently fearless women. They had a low opinion of his fighting courage. Anne Bonney unkindly said as much to Rackham in his cell before his execution. Perhaps she was right. He is described as engaging with a French man of war but is also captured easily by a privateer off Negril Point, Jamaica. It could be that Rackham was simply weak. Perhaps the crew of the *Ranger* had put Vane adrift and voted in good-looking and raffish Rackham as captain because he was less likely to be reckless than Vane. Quartermasters (Rackham's rank before he replaced Vane) were expected to counterbalance the captain in a pirate-ship democracy. Rather than leading Vane's crew against him, it could be that Rackham simply fell into the role. The rest of Vane's career is pretty crackpot. Their former captain,[14] Jennings, had accepted a pardon from Woodes Rogers. Vane had refused: that's how he became captain. But once in the role, he refused to follow the pirates' code or rules and ran his ship on lines a great deal less democratic than they had expected. Vane had been reckless. He was friends with and celebrated a kind of bacchanalia with Blackbeard Teach and his crew in the autumn of 1718.[15] If the crew of the *Ranger* knew that determined Royal Navy ships were looking for them (as Teach was about to discover) while an amnesty was on offer in Nassau, New Providence, they must have known they were at a fork in the road. The psychopathic and terrifying Blackbeard and his cruel, torturing friend Vane, both failing to follow the pirates' code, intimidating and terrorizing their crews with as much gusto as they attacked shipping, represented one future (short, nasty, rum-fuelled and wild), while dapper Calico Jack Rackham would take them back to Nassau and peace in which to enjoy their gains. For the time being, they made the right choice. Within six weeks of the decision by the crew of the *Ranger* to follow Rackham, it seemed justified. Blackbeard's head was hanging off Lieutenant Maynard's bowsprit. Within six months Vane was a shipwrecked sailor in the Honduras. Vane was unlucky enough to be rescued by a ship's captain who recognized him and took him prisoner. Later that year Rackham had squandered his peace in Nassau and went a-pirating again with his newly besotted lover Anne Bonney at his side. By November 1720 Rackham too was dead, executed after his trial in Spanish Town. Mary Read was in the final months of the pregnancy and incarceration which would end in her death from fever early in 1721.

Anne and Mary sound as fierce and determined as any pirate a sailor was likely to meet in the Caribbean. But their circumstances were very specific. Even apparently free men and women have a narrow palette of choices of action, depending on their circumstances and – frankly – their intelligence. The experiences of Blackbeard's women suggest that the women associated with pirates would have needed to be immensely brave just to survive. Whether Anne Bonney and Mary Read were dangerous in the sense of being prime movers of attacks on other ships is open to debate. That they fought bravely when they had to is certain. And both were constant, in their own way. Mary died without uttering her lover's name. Anne had two children with Rackham (probably) and eight more with her Charleston husband, suggesting she was more interested in reproduction than piracy.

7

VIKINGS

There seems to me to be a natural conjunction between Teach's overt sexual savagery, as reported by Johnson/ Defoe, and reports about those earliest of recorded Atlantic pirates, Vikings. How? From Johnson/Defoe's text it seems Blackbeard's story is derived from the account of one of Teach's companions. It therefore carries some conviction for the reader. If Johnson/Defoe's description of Teach is hearsay, it is compelling and contemporary hearsay. Imagine you'd spoken to a man who'd met bin Laden – that's the measure both of proximity and of infamy. Bin Laden is of course without equal in our period. Do Blackbeard and his band of pirates have any rivals? I think they do, but in an earlier age: Vikings. And there exists a contemporary description of Viking behaviour and rite by a trustworthy outside source.

In the early English period the very word Viking (or wicing) meant pirate, and far into the later centuries men were said to be going a-wicing – they were off robbing. The original Vikings from the period roughly circa AD 750–1060 were ferocious, persistent, well armed and such a pest that large areas of modern France (Normandy) and England (in the form of the Danegeld tax) were handed over to their control in an attempt to pacify them. From the eighth century on there are descriptions of Viking fleets maraud-ing the English, Irish and French countryside for months and of local chiefs and officials organizing payoffs to get rid of them. Charles III of France paid 5,000 silver livres to the Viking leader Rollo (or Hrolf Ganger as he was known before his name was Latinized). How very similar this is to Teach and his relationship with Charleston – could it be that the warm and wet British Isles and Atlantic French provinces appeared to the Vikings much as the East Coast of what is now the United States appeared to our ancestors, Teach's generation and those immediately before it? That is, Christian England and France was a land rich in resources, weakly defended and free for the plucking? Like the British Americans in the Carolinas, Charlemagne's children and grandchildren were in no position to defend France. Off the continental mainland and a relatively easy sail from home for the Vikings, the British Isles were even more exposed, with a long vulnerable coastline, rich monasteries ripe for plunder, poor communications and weak defences. Britain and Ireland were a series of kingdoms ruled by men struggling for power with each other and their neighbours. Unlike in the case of Teach, unfortunately, Anglo-Saxon society of the period wasn't strongly structured politically; there was no settled authority, no orderly world outside to send an avenging Captain Maynard (or in the case of the Mediterranean pirates we began with, even a Caesar) to put an end to the Viking pirates' adventures. Western Europe was too weak and the Vikings too strong and determined for a power struggle. It was rather a case of, 'what accommodation could be made?' The kings of what were to become England and France made deals with the invaders, just as the citizens of Charleston did with Blackbeard. In France, Normandy became the home of the Vikings – William the Conquerer was the fourth-generation descendant of Viking Rollo. Rollo was handed the territory in the west of France on the basis he was recognized as a separate duke (actually a term from the Middle Ages – Rollo would have been called a Jarl by his contemporaries) but was nominally inferior to the French king in Paris, Charles III (known as Charles the Simple). According to a later chronicler, as a sign of this 'fealty' Rollo was meant to kiss Charles the Simple's foot, which he did in a comic fashion, tipping Charles head over arse, to the amusement of his Viking companions. In England the Viking claims ended with the installation of a Danish king, Cnut, though one view is that the real resolution of the Viking raids on England was the invasion and accession to the throne of the Conqueror or Bastard William of Normandy. William's supporters, court, bishops and soldiers were all the very close descendants of Vikings. The Viking age is one in which the pirates won.

But England, France and Ireland weren't the only recipients of unwelcome visits from Viking pirates. Their raids made the coast of Brittany untenable for the Bretons, who withdrew inland; Vikings occupied the Channel Islands, invaded the Mediterranean as far as Sicily. They may have been in a very literal sense the ancestors of Channel Islander and Malouin privateers, the fathers of Corsican and Barbary pirates. One of the Eastern Roman emperors had Viking bodyguards (just as many Roman emperors had German personal bodyguards). Vikings traded with Arabs and travelled deep into Russia, and it is the extraordinary conjunction of these two groups which gives us an insight into the social life of Viking pirates of the Rus in AD 921, the height of Viking power. This was the same year during which the Battle of Madlon, between Anglo-Saxons and Vikings on the river Blackwater in Essex, took place. Ibn Fadlan was an emissary from the Caliph of Baghdad. Sent abroad over some scandal at home he fell in with Vikings while travelling in Russia. He reports on their social arrangements and funeral rites, sometimes with an amused tone, as an adult might look at the antics of children, sometimes aghast at their savagery and what his Muslim sensibility saw as their 'dirtiness'. What follows is a distillation of the numerous translations of Fadlan's account. Fadlan stayed with the Vikings for some time, and what he saw of the Vikings' sexual mores has a striking resemblance to the behaviour of Blackbeard's pirates. This shouldn't be surprising. If pirates were an outsider society with their own rules and customs, those rules seem to have been developed to indicate the strength and power of the leader, and the rites seem to use women and sexuality to define the respect in which he was held. This would be true for pirates of any age. Fadlan tells us:

They are the dirtiest people. They do not wash them-selves, any more than if they were wild asses. They come from their country in the North and anchor their ships in the Volga River. Each man has a couch, where he sits with the beautiful slave girls he has for sale. Here he is as likely as not to enjoy one of them while another Viking looks on. At times several of them will be thus engaged, each in full view of the others. Sometimes a buyer will come to a house to purchase a girl, and find her master embracing her, and he will not give the slave over until she has satisfied him [. . .]

I was told that when their chiefs die, they consume them with fire. When I heard that one of their leaders had died, I decided to see this for myself, and I did. The dead man was first put in a grave, over which a roof was erected, for the space of ten days. During this time they made his funeral clothes. When a rich man dies, they bring together his goods, and divide them into three parts. The first part is for his family. The second is for the garments they make. And with the third they purchase strong drink, for the day when one of his girl slaves resigns herself to death, and allows herself to be burned with her master. His family asks his slaves, Which one of you will die with him? And one will answer, I will. From the moment she says this, she may not go back. Regarding this dead man, a slave girl answered "I will." She was then entrusted to two other girls, who accompanied her everywhere she went. They even washed her feet with their own hands. Then they began to get things ready for the dead man; making his clothes and everything else that should be done, while the slave who was going to die drank and sang every day happily and joyfully.

When the day came that the dead man should be burned together with his slave, I went to the river where the ship lay. It had been hauled up on land and supported by four posts of birch and other wood. Around it was arranged what looked like a large pile of wood. The ship was then drawn up and placed on the wood. People began to go to and fro and spoke words which I did not understand, but the corpse still lay in the grave from which they had not yet taken it. They then brought a bier which was placed in the ship; they covered it with tapestries and with cushions of Byzantine brocade.

Then an old woman, whom they call the Angel of Death, came and spread these hangings on the bier. She is in charge of embalming the dead man and preparing him and it is she who kills the girl. The one I saw was a strongly-built and grim figure. When they came to the grave they removed the earth from the wood and removed the wood as well.

They then removed the loin cloth which he was wearing when he died. I noticed that the body had turned black, owing to the coldness of the ground. They had put with him in the grave nabidh [which is sometimes translated as wine, sometimes as an intoxicating draft or sleeping draught. From its use later in the story, Fadal must mean the latter], fruit and a lute, all of which they now took out. The corpse did not smell at all and nothing but the colour of his flesh had changed. They then clothed him in drawers and trousers, boots and tunic, and a brocade mantle with gold buttons on it. They placed a cap made of brocade and sable on his head. They carried him into a tent which stood on the ship, and laid him on the tapestry and propped him up with the cushions. They then brought nabidh, fruit and sweet-smelling herbs and laid these beside him. Next they brought bread, meat and onions and threw these beside him. Next they took two horses which they caused to run until they were sweating, after which they cut them in pieces with a sword and threw their flesh into the ship.

Then they brought two cows, which they also cut into pieces and threw them in. The slave woman who wished to be killed went to and fro from one tent to another, and the man of each tent had intercourse with her and said, 'Tell your master that I have done this out of love for him.' It was now Friday afternoon and they took the slave away to something which looked like the frame of a door. Then she put her legs on the hands of the men and was thus lifted, so that she was above the top of the door-frame, and she said something . . . [this was done three times]. Then they gave her a chicken and she cut off its head and threw it away. Then they took the hen and threw it into the ship.

Then I asked what she had done and my interpreter answered: The first time they lifted her up she said, Look, I see my mother and father; the second time she said, Look, I see all my dead relations sitting together; the third time she said, Look, I see my master sitting in paradise and paradise is beautiful and green, and together with him are men and young boys. He called to me, so let me go to him. They then took her to the ship. She then took off two arm-bands which she had on and gave them to the old woman who was called the Angel of Death, who was the one who would kill her; she also took off two ankle-rings which she wore and gave them to the two girls who were in attendance on her and who are the daughters of the woman called the Angel of Death. Then they took her to the ship, but did not allow her to enter the tent on it.

Then came men who had shields and staves, and gave her a beaker of nabidh. She sang over it and drained it. The interpreter said to me, she now takes farewell of her friends. Then she was given another beaker. She took this and sang for a long time, but the old woman warned her that she should drink quickly and go into the tent where her master lay.

When I looked at her, she seemed bemused, she wanted to go into the tent and put her head between it and the ship, then the old woman took her hand and made her enter the tent and went in with her. At this moment the men began to beat upon their shields, in order to drown out the noise of her cries, which might stop other slave girls from seeking death with their masters in the future. They laid her down and seized her hands and feet. The old woman known as the Angel of Death knotted a rope around her neck and handed the ends to two men to pull. Then with a broad dagger she stabbed her between the ribs while the men strangled her. Thus the slave girl died.

A naked senior member of the family of the dead man drew near with a piece of wood and lit the ship. The ship was soon aflame, as was the couch, the dead man, the girl, and everything in it. One of the Norsemen said to me, You Arabs are stupid. You would take a man who is the most revered and beloved among men, and cast him into the ground, to be devoured by creeping things and worms. We, on the other hand, burn him in a twinkling, so that he instantly, without a moment's delay, enters into Paradise.

One wonders what would have happened if a slave girl had not volunteered. This seems to me to be very like Teach's treatment of his wife (and for all we know serial wives – Johnson/Defoe said there were many). The woman and her sexuality is used as a bonding device for the warrior males. What else is Teach doing when he asks his crew to have intercourse with his teenage bride? Binding the men to him makes them a viable outsider society, an alternative order to which the pirates can relate. Of course piracy is about a kind of freedom, about chaos, money, drink and excess, but it seems to me to be more about this 'alternative society' or alternative order than anything else. Why else take the risks? Why else fight for gold you can't spend? Gang life has its own rules and attractions, pirate-gang life no less than any other. Young (I mean under 40) men appear to have a profound drive towards this highly bonded, group behaviour and it may be that psychopathic characters like Teach exploit this, even to the extent that in Viking pirate society it had become bound into the formal social mores. What was the rape or even the ritualized killing of a woman to compare to this benefit? It cost the Viking pirates and Teach's pirates almost nothing. And the benefit to the leader and to the group – the establishment of a tightly bonded and aggressive male group with a firmly founded leadership structure – was enormous. This is exactly the sort of group which would follow its leader where others wouldn't and would overcome other less ferocious groups, like merchant ships' crews or coastal villagers.

8

PIRATES AGROUND

Though piracy remains with us, the reign of terror of Blackbeard, Vane, Rackham and their like was brief. Though the golden age of Spanish Main pirates lasted from the latter part of the seventeenth century until the early part of the eighteenth, its high point was in the first couple of decades of the Georgian century. Historian Marcus Rediker estimates there were one to two thousand pirates active from 1716 to 1726. That seems reasonable. Of course we only know details about a few of them, and those we do know about come to our attention either because of their notoriety and inclusion in books like Johnson/Defoe's *History of the Pyrates*, or through newspaper or court reports of their crimes. We don't have most of their names. Rediker goes on to suggest that they were drawn from the lower orders of society. Perhaps they were but it wasn't universal. Stede Bonnet and Anne Bonney weren't. Rediker puts pirates' ages between 18 and 50. Less obviously he estimates their average age to be older than that of Royal Navy or merchant seamen. In *The Pirates' Who's Who*, Philip Gosse goes further and suggests pirates were the best crews and the best sailors of their day. It is often repeated but I think it may be a mistake. Teach's men weren't better sailors or braver than Captain Maynard. In his last battle Teach is said to have run aground on purpose. Perhaps he did, perhaps he didn't. He seems to have run ships aground regularly. It was an occupational hazard for sailors of the period, but there were plenty of seamen who didn't strand their ships, which is as likely to lead to the breaking up of the vessel or drowning of the crew as it is to protect them from military ships' gunfire.[16] Blackbeard's crew, like Vane and many other pirates who ended up in court, appear to have come there via their navigational inadequacies as much as any other route. I don't suggest for a moment that men who wandered the Spanish Main in unhandy tubby barques, lacking more than the most rudimentary charts, crewed by argumentative ne'er-do-wells and laden down with gold and guns, were simply bad sailors. Of course they weren't. But Royal Navy and privateer ships – in other words, ships under discipline – seem to have fared better. No one can claim Stede Bonnet was a good sailor, or advised by good sailors. If pirates weren't bad sailors they weren't particularly good ones either.

The Spanish Main pirates' nemesis arrived in 1718 in the form of a privateer, Captain Woodes Rogers. His presence (or rather the presence of someone like him) had been sought of King George by that vigorous protector of royal property, prerogative and privilege in the Americas, the

Lieutenant Governor of Virginia, Alexander Spotswood. Spotswood was from a royalist military family which had prospered under the Restoration. He was an energetic leader and administrator of the American colony and a loyal servant to the British government. Allowing local administrations to make private arrangements with pirates, or for that matter Indian chiefs, or even with the hierarchy of the local Church of England was anathema to him.[17] Spotswood wanted to make the English legacy in North America a well-run, efficient and legal regime (by the standards of its day). To Spotswood this meant curbing the powers of the colonials and re-establishing absolute crown control, making settlements with the Indians, regularizing land grants so that they were made to settlers not speculators and clearing the colony of pirates. To this last end Spotswood petitioned London for military aid. King George's government's response was to have the well-known privateer Woodes Rogers installed in Nassau. The more or less corrupt administrations of the Carolinas did not request military aid against the pirates. It was also Spotswood rather than Charles Eden (Governor of North Carolina) who later sent Maynard to confront Teach. Eden was cuttingly described by a North Carolina resident as able to raise a posse to pursue honest men but not Teach. The *Oxford Dictionary of National Biography* states, 'the greatest controversy attached to Eden was a possible association with Edward Teach, the notorious pirate Blackbeard. Pirates had long operated on the southern coasts of North America, using the colonies' harbours to refit their vessels, hide, and rest . . . While the neighbouring colonies of Virginia and South Carolina mounted campaigns to thwart the pirates, Eden remained suspiciously inactive. Further questions were asked when a letter from Tobias Knight, the secretary of the governor's council, declaring Eden's desire to meet with Blackbeard was found on the pirate's dead body . . .' At that time New Providence (i.e. the Bahamian Island containing Nassau) was part of the Virginia colony and nominally under Spotswood's control. In fact it was under no one's control and was regularly attacked by French and Spanish as well as by pirates. New Providence was described in contemporary documents as a 'nest of pirates'. I imagine the atmosphere was something like that of Beirut in the 1980s. You knew which group you belonged to, but that never meant it wasn't easy to be captured, robbed or tortured. Charles Vane and Blackbeard used it as a base. Pirates strode the streets without fear of arrest. The solution the British Crown chose for this problem was to sub-let the governorship of the island to Captain Woodes Rogers, passing him very broad powers to suppress piracy and grant pardons to those pirates willing to give up their sea-robbing livelihoods. It was a variation of colonial government – the classic privateering solution applied to a colony but it did have the advantage of transferring power out to where it was needed.

Woodes Rogers wasn't new to privateering. He had made a kind of privateering world tour between 1708 and 1711, capturing prizes and invading Spanish colonies. He even visited remote spots like Guam and the Galapagos Islands. The expedition made Woodes Rogers famous and, as a result, he published a history of his own privateering adventures, *A Cruising Voyage Round the World.*

Rogers arrived in Nassau in 1718 and offered the King's Pardon to those who would take it. He is reported to have been received ashore by enthusiastic pirates firing their muskets into the air – something which suggests that at least a proportion of the pirates were pleased to see him. Of course, many may have 'joined' their pirate ships in a more or less unwilling fashion and been heartily relieved to leave them. On Rogers' arrival Blackbeard and Vane quit the island. Rogers rebuilt the town's fort, organized a militia and a town council, and began to re-develop trade links. He also organized privateering expeditions to hunt down the pirates who hadn't taken the pardon. Woodes Rogers was making a concerted attempt to overcome the viable outsider society needed by pirates and replace it with the rule of law. Of course, it was early eighteenth-century law – when former pirates reverted to their old trade, Rogers had them tried and hanged in public. Meanwhile, off the Carolinas, Spotswood's man Maynard captured and beheaded Teach. In the Honduras Vane shipwrecked himself, ensuring he would be returned to Jamaica and hanged. By the end of the year Rackham would be dead too.

Woodes Rogers' presence in Nassau and Spotswood's in Virginia put an end to the period of piracy in the Spanish Main which is so lovingly described in the *History of the Pyrates*, whether that book was written by Defoe or the otherwise unknown Captain Johnson. There's no evidence that Woodes Rogers ever met Defoe. But *History of the Pyrates* or not, Woodes Rogers has another extraordinary literary connection with Defoe. In his *Voyage* Woodes Rogers tells of finding a man marooned in what are now known as the Galapagos Islands. He describes the man as having with him:

> ... a firelock, some powder, bullets and tobacco, a hatchet, a knife, a kettle, a Bible, some practical pieces, and his mathematical instruments and books. He diverted and provided for himself as well as he could, but for the first eight months had to bear up against melancholy, and the terror of being left alone in such a desolate place ... After he had conquered his melancholy, he diverted himself sometimes with cutting his name on trees, and of the time of his being left, and continuance there ... When his clothes were worn out he made himself a coat and a cap of goat skins, which he stitched together with little thongs of the same, that he cut with his knife. He had no other needle but a nail; and when his knife was worn to the back he made others, as well as he could, of some iron hoops that were left ashore, which he beat thin and ground upon stones. Having some linen cloth by him, he sewed him some shirts with a nail and, stitched them with the worsted of his old stockings, which he pulled out on purpose. He had his last shirt on when we found him on the island.

The man in the cap and coat of goatskins was a castaway, Alexander Selkirk. Defoe fictionalized his story in a book entitled *The Life and Strange Surprising Adventures of Robinson Crusoe of York, Mariner: who lived Eight and Twenty Years, all alone in an uninhabited Island on the coast of America, near the Mouth of the Great River of Orinoco; Having been cast on Shore by Shipwreck, wherein all the Men perished but himself. With An Account how he was at last as strangely deliver'd by Pirates. Written by Himself.* In other words, Selkirk, rescued by privateer Woodes Rogers, was the model for Daniel Defoe's Robinson Crusoe. If Woodes Rogers didn't manage to rid the world of piracy, in his writing he managed at least to introduce the subject of the first novel in English to its creator.

NOTES

1. i.e. Burmese. I believe China is the only country which refers to Burma by its junta name of Myanmar.
2. Buccaneer is derived from 'boucan', a form of dried meat and sometimes the name of a type of barbeque.
3. Among others, the expert on pirates and former National Maritime Museum curator David Cordingly has dismissed the long-accepted theory that Defoe anonymously wrote *Captain Johnson's General History of the Pyrates.* Cordingly may well be right but, if he is, it means there is an enormously talented writer of literary non-fiction of the eighteenth century of whom we know nothing except this work. Until he is discovered, and bearing in mind Defoe's other seafaring works, I will follow the US publisher Dover and many other reputable editors and treat Defoe and Johnson as one and the same.
4. In French, 'faire la corse' formerly meant to go sea-robbing. 'Corse' here refers to Corsica, in French culture the traditional home of brigands and sea robbers, the original corsairs.

5. A pink was a form of small square-rigged trading vessel, characteristic of the Mediterranean.

6. A hundred years later Charles Dickens would work there as a shorthand reporter, following in his father's footsteps. The elder Dickens – an Admiralty clerk – had acquired the skill while imprisoned in the Marshalsea for debt.

7. Compare Richardson's history to Hervey Cleckley's checklist for Anti Social Personality Disorder (Cleckley, *The Mask of Sanity*: New York, New American Library, 1988):

1. Considerable superficial charm and average or above average intelligence.

2. Absence of delusions and other signs of irrational thinking.

3. Absence of anxiety or other 'neurotic' symptoms; considerable poise, calmness, and verbal facility.

4. Unreliability, disregard for obligations, no sense of responsibility in matters of little and great import.

5. Untruthfulness and insincerity.

6. Antisocial behavior which is inadequately motivated and poorly planned, seeming to stem from an inexplicable impulsiveness.

7. Inadequately motivated antisocial behavior.

8. Poor judgment and failure to learn from experience.

9. Pathological egocentricity. Total self-centeredness, incapacity for real love and attachment.

10. General poverty of deep and lasting emotions.

11. Lack of any true insight, inability to see oneself as others do.

12. Ingratitude for any special considerations, kindness, and trust.

13. Fantastic and objectionable behavior after drinking and sometimes even when not drinking; vulgarity, rudeness, quick mood shifts; fond of pranks.

14. No history of genuine suicide attempts.

15. An impersonal, trivial, and poorly integrated sex life.

16. Failure to have a life plan and to live in any ordered way, unless it be one promoting self-defeat.

8. Navy Records Society 1910/12.

9. Comparisons of value are difficult across long periods of time. Eighteenth-century men and women did not generally draw salaries and house prices are not a reliable subject for comparison. Instead I chose beer. A gallon of beer (according to the Global Price and Income History Group) would have been 8 or 9 pence in 1690. £1,000 would have bought 27,000 gallons or 216,000 pints. Pints of beer in London in 2007 cost approximately £4, meaning Avery's sailors received £864,000 at 2007 prices for robbing the Grand Mughal's ships.

10. See http://www.oldbaileyonline.org/ for more examples of extraordinary punishments for trifling crimes.

11. He means the War of the Spanish Succession, which ended finally in 1714 and had lasted for over ten years.

12. In other words, after the death of Queen Anne and five years after the Treaty of Utrecht, which was the formal end of the War of the Spanish Succession.

13. In other words, receive a reprieve.

14. i.e. the one before Vane.

15. In 'The Social World of Anglo-American Pirates' (*William and Mary Quarterly*, 1981).

16. If you lightened a ship to reduce draft and sailed into shallows it would be difficult for a military ship to follow without also abandoning her guns.

17. One of the disputes that dogged his administration was his insistence on Royal Prerogative over appointment of a local bishop.

BIBLIOGRAPHY

Further Reading

Cordingly, David, *Life Among the Pirates: Romance and Reality*, London: Little, Brown, 1995

Defoe, Daniel, *Captain Johnson's General History of the Pyrates*, New York: Dover Publications, 1999

Defoe, Daniel, *Robinson Crusoe*, Harmondsworth: Penguin, 1970

Exquemelin, Alexander, *The Buccaneers of America*, NewYork: Dover Publications, 2003

Gosse, Philip, *The History of Piracy*, New York: Dover Publications, 2007

Marine Research Society, *The Pirates Own Book: Authentic Narratives of the Most Celebrated Sea Robbers*, NewYork: Dover Publications, 1993

Rediker, Marcus, *Villains of All Nations: Atlantic Pirates in the Golden Age*, London: Verso Books, 2004

Rogers, Woodes, *A Cruising Voyage Round the World*, Crabtree, Oregon: Narrative Press, 2004

Sanders, Richard, *If a Pirate I Must Be: The True Story of Bartholomew Roberts, King of the Caribbean*, London: Aurum, 2007

Talty, Stephan, *Empire of Blue Water: Henry Morgan and the Pirates Who Ruled the Caribbean Waves*, London: Simon & Schuster, 2007

Websites

www.piratesinfo.com
Wide-ranging site on piracy that includes short biographical articles about famous pirates (Stede Bonnet, Henry Morgan, Blackbeard et al.) and online texts of classic works on pirates.

http://en.wikipedia.org/wiki/Piracy
The main Wikipedia article on piracy leads through to a host of other articles on individual pirates, pirates in fiction etc.

www.thepirateking.com
Online biographies of pirates, gallery of pirate weaponry, short dictionary of nautical terminology etc.

www.oldbaileyonline.org
Online accounts of thousands of criminal trials held at London's central criminal court between 1674 and 1834, including a number for piracy.

INDEX